Against the Christians

Patristic Studies

Gerald Bray
General Editor

Vol. 1

PETER LANG
New York • Washington, D.C./Baltimore • Boston • Bern
Frankfurt am Main • Berlin • Brussels • Vienna • Canterbury

Jeffrey W. Hargis

Against the Christians

The Rise of Early
Anti-Christian Polemic

PETER LANG
New York • Washington, D.C./Baltimore • Boston • Bern
Frankfurt am Main • Berlin • Brussels • Vienna • Canterbury

Library of Congress Cataloging-in-Publication Data

Hargis, Jeffrey W.
Against the Christians: the rise
of early anti-Christian polemic / Jeffrey W. Hargis.
p. cm. — (Patristic studies; vol. 1)
Includes bibliographical references and index.
1. Christianity—Controversial literature. 2. Philosophy, Ancient. 3. Rome—
Religion. 4. Christianity and other religions—Roman. 5. Church
history—Primitive and early church, ca. 30–600. I. Title. II. Series:
Patristic studies (Peter Lang Publishing); vol. 1.
BR160.3.H37   270.1—dc21   98-25584
ISBN 0-8204-4156-2
ISSN 1094–6217

Die Deutsche Bibliothek-CIP-Einheitsaufnahme

Hargis, Jeffrey W.:
Against the Christians: the rise
of early anti-christian polemic / Jeffrey W. Hargis.
–New York; Washington, D.C./Baltimore; Boston; Bern;
Frankfurt am Main; Berlin; Brussels; Vienna; Canterbury: Lang.
(Patristic studies; Vol. 1)
ISBN 0-8204-4156-2

Cover design by Nona Reuter

The paper in this book meets the guidelines for permanence and durability
of the Committee on Production Guidelines for Book Longevity
of the Council of Library Resources.

© 1999 Peter Lang Publishing, Inc., New York

Printed in the United States of America

To Gerard S. Sloyan

Teacher, Mentor, Friend

Acknowledgments

For making this work possible, I extend gratitude and honor first to Merilyn, my wife. Her love, support and confidence in me were invaluable and cannot be adequately acknowledged.

Many thanks are also due to my instructors at Temple University, whose encouragement and direction made this project a reality. Special thanks go to Dr. Gerard Sloyan, without whose wisdom and practical assistance this book would not have been written. Thanks to Dr. Vasiliki Limberis for reminding me that ancient texts were not written in a historical or cultural vacuum and for encouraging the creative aspect of historical study. Dr. Robert Wright's practical instruction in the "how to" of scholarship was invaluable, as were his extraordinarily high standards for precision in both thinking and writing.

Acknowledgment and thanks go to my friend and colleague, Dr. M. James Sawyer of Western Seminary, whose many valuable contributions to the writing of this book go far beyond his thorough review of the manuscript.

Quotations from *Against the Galileans* are reprinted by permission of the publishers and the Loeb Classical Library from JULIAN: VOLUME III translated by W.C. Wright, Cambridge, Mass.: Harvard University Press, 1923.

Quotations from *City of God* are reproduced by permission of Penguin Books Ltd. from Augustine, *City of God*, pp. 421, 886–888, translated by Henry Bettenson, Penguin Classics, London, 1972. Translation copyright © Henry Bettenson, 1972; introduction copyright © John O'Meara, 1984.

Quotations from *Contra Celsum* are reprinted by permission of Cambridge University Press from *Origen: Contra Celsum*, translated by Henry Chadwick, Cambridge University Press, 1953.

Table of Contents

1 Defining the Christian "Other": From Persecution
    to Polemic   1

2 Celsus and the "Revolt Against the Community"   17

3 Celsus, Plato, and the Gods   41

4 Porphyry and the Polemic of Universalism   63

5 Julian the Apostate and the Politics of Hellenism   91

6 Julian and the Bounded God   107

7 Negotiating the Pagan-Christian Divide   129

   Notes   139

   Select Bibliography   155

   Index   167

1

Defining the Christian "Other": From Persecution to Polemic

The fact that Christianity emerged within the cultural milieu of Roman Hellenism is no longer a matter of debate in the scholarship of early Christianity or of late antiquity. Gone are the days in which scholars viewed the advance of Christianity as a fledgling faith wrestling its way into power from the outside, replacing in the process a dying Hellenism or a corrupt paganism while introducing a radically new worldview into the Mediterranean basin. Instead, a set of continuities is now assumed in the study of early Christianity, continuity both with Judaism (particularly in the realm of New Testament studies) and with Græco-Roman culture. The patristic conception of Christians as a "third race," distinct from both Jews and pagans, has been effectively replaced by the consensus that Christianity evolved more naturally from its Jewish and Hellenistic ancestry, a domestic model rather than a religious import. The eventual triumph of Christianity was at least partially a result of, not simply an alternative to, developments occurring within pagan culture and religion from the first to the fourth centuries CE. The growth of the church and the Christianization of the Roman Empire did not constitute a foreign invasion, but rather the emergence of a naturally-born child to maturity.

The implications of this emergence are still being worked out. One of the earlier aspects of Christianity to be identified as a child of Hellenism was its conscious (and sometimes not-so-conscious) adoption of Platonist philosophical categories; one of the more recent, its adoption of Græco-Roman rhetoric. By introducing sociological methodologies unfamiliar to most scholars of early Christianity, Rodney Stark[1] has added a new dimension to the project. Explaining the rise of Christianity has become a project approached with renewed vigor at the close of the twentieth century.

One of the relatively unexplored regions relating to this project consists of the corpus of early anti-Christian literature. This corpus includes the polemic writings of an otherwise unknown author named Celsus in the late second or early third century CE, of the Neoplatonic philosopher Porphyry in about 270, and of the last pagan emperor Julian in 362–363. As scholars seek to document the gestation of Christianity within its Græco-Roman womb, this literature presents a special set of problems. The anti-Christian treatises, like virtually all polemic literature, sought to accentuate the differences between the polemicists and their opponents while minimizing the similarities. Of course, it is in the very nature of polemic interchange that the differences between opposing sides become exaggerated and their similarities downplayed. Just listen to the rhetoric of any ideologically-conscious candidate for office, for example, or read the fund-raising literature of political organizations attempting to frighten their constituencies with the specter of a right- or left-wing takeover. The genre of polemic emphasizes and often exaggerates difference, sometimes to humorous extremes. However, the boundaries between pagan and Christian were not always as clear as the polemicists portrayed them. The boundaries could be manipulated by either side according to the needs of the rhetorical moment. This fact offers opportunities as well as obstacles to the scholar investigating the relationship between the Christian child and its pagan parent.

At the same time, it must be noted that the pagan literature is not uniform in its emphasis on difference. This observation assists us somewhat in tracing the development of the polemicists' rhetorical strategies over time. As we will see, the rhetoric of difference in Celsus' *True Doctrine* is particularly exaggerated, a fact lost on many interpreters who seek to reconstruct the church of the late second century by way of Celsus' polemic. In contrast, the anti-Christian works of Porphyry and Julian actually display a conscious acceptance of some elements of Christianity, even as they use these very elements in a strategy of attack and not as points to be conceded to their opponents. The specifics of this strategy will be observed as we proceed; suffice it to say for now that in each polemic work, even that of Celsus, there are identifiable congruences between pagan and Christian thought. These congruences undermine the rhetoric of difference that is otherwise intrinsic to the genre; thus even the type of literature that most demanded a rhetoric of radical difference could not maintain such a rhetoric completely. This fact should alert us to investigate more seriously the religious, cultural and intellectual proximity of the Christian and pagan universes.

To be sure, this proximity is more clearly visible from the Christian side; Christian apologists had a greater stake in a rhetoric of similarity than did their pagan opponents. A common apologetic strategy, to which Tatian and Tertullian were prominent exceptions, was to downplay at many points the differences between their own beliefs and those of their persecutors. The tendency since Justin for Christians to claim Plato as their philosophical ancestor was only one of the more well-known apologetic tactics. At times it was also advantageous to present Christ as similar to pagan gods and heroes in order to present him as a reasonable object of worship. Naturally, the apologists spelled out the unique aspects of their faith with determination even as they condemned polytheism. Often, however, Christian writers found it in their interest to emphasize similarity with the surrounding culture and with pagan religion, especially when they were under the threat of persecution.

The pagan polemicists had no such interest. For them the attribution of "otherness" was standard practice; Celsus' work, for example, exaggerates Christian difference to such a degree that his critique provides at times only a caricature of his opponents. But although the construction of rhetorical boundaries between Christianity and paganism was a vital element in the anti-Christian literary project, the three polemicists did not always use the same building materials. Thus it is interesting to see Porphyry and Julian, in contrast to Celsus, occasionally adopting and signaling agreement with specific elements of Christian belief. This characteristic, out of place as it appears in the genre of polemic, reveals many of the points of contact between Christian and pagan thought. More precisely, these elements of agreement enable us to glimpse, however imperfectly, a few of the threads of understanding that the two sides shared in an often bitter debate. These threads, were we able to weave them together again in their totality, would allow us to view the tapestry of the world view common to both pagan and Christian in late antiquity.

Even if such a reconstruction were possible, it would be beyond the purpose of this book; the goals of this study are much more modest. This book examines the extant pagan anti-Christian polemic literature with a view toward discovering the strategies by which the polemicists attempted to marginalize a religious opponent steadily increasing in numbers, sophistication and power. In the process it identifies and describes the polemic boundaries between pagan and Christian as the authors constructed them, boundaries which shifted significantly between the time of Celsus and the reign of Julian. It is the construction of these boundaries, with their varying degrees of ambiguity and fluidity, that enable us to detect the rhetorical strategies that the pagan polemicists employed against their Christian opponents.

Although the anti-Christian literature reveals some common assumptions the two sides shared, it goes without saying that the differences between pagans and Christians were profound and that both polemic and apologetic were grounded in substantial disagreement on a vast array of issues. It is, in fact, such wide-ranging conflict that allows us to see the occasional rhetorical and substantive convergences in the first place.

Take for example the familiar battle line between Christian monotheism and pagan polytheism. What may at first glance be regarded as a clear disagreement between the Christian "one" and the pagan "many" was much more ambiguous than it might seem. In the first place, a pagan "monotheism" had existed long before Christians began to make an issue of the oneness of the divine; the concept was still undergoing significant development over the time period covered in this study. It is therefore possible to view the polemic over this issue not as a fundamental disagreement on the number of gods but as a series of attempts to define the shape of the monotheism that ultimately was to emerge from the struggle. Further, the fact that Christians worshiped Jesus in addition to God the Father made Christian monotheism an ambiguous issue indeed. While such ambiguity eventually followed the church into the fourth-century councils, it was also an issue in its earlier apologetic. The deity of Jesus made it necessary for Christians to defend themselves against the charge of inconsistency from pagan opponents who pointed to their worship of at least two divine beings. Defining the mathematics of Christian monotheism was not only a problem for the later conciliar age, it was an early apologetic task of the first order.

A further examination of the polemic reveals more concrete implications of the pagans' rejection of Christian monotheism. One of these implications, perhaps obscured by Western cultural distance from agrarian society, was a profound disagreement over the control of natural forces. Greek and Roman and other polytheisms allocated the management of the natural universe to the care of specific deities most suited to carry out their functions for the benefit of humanity. How, then, could the Christian God, distant as he was from the day to day contingencies of human survival, perform the lifegiving functions traditionally assigned to the gods of nature? It is possible that Christian evangelists were developing an apologetic response to this issue as early as the first century.

> In the past, [God] let all nations go their own way. Yet he has not left himself without testimony: He has shown kindness by giving you rain from heaven and crops in their seasons; he provides you with plenty of food and fills your hearts with joy.[2]

The early pagan objection to Christian monotheism was not simply a dispute over heavenly mathematics. It was more fundamentally an argument concerning the relationship of deity to nature and of the provision for human needs. It was an objection that Christian apologists took seriously.

In this excursus on monotheism we must also remember that Christians by and large accepted the actual existence of the gods. They relegated them, of course, to the category of evil "daemons" that were not worthy of worship. But it would have been difficult for Christians to deny outright the reality of those beings that virtually everyone (true atheists, if there were any, excepted) believed were real. Once we understand the ambiguities involved in an issue so fundamental to pagan-Christian discourse as monotheism, we may shift our focus from the explicit rhetoric of difference to the identification of more subtle but nonetheless common interests. The situation was not unlike that of a married couple arguing over the placement of the living room furniture: no matter how vehement the argument, the disagreement stems from the fact of common ownership. The real issue is one of control; so it was with the religious, cultural and philosophical "furniture" of Roman Hellenism. For our purposes, what is important is that the disagreement between pagans and Christians on many issues was substantial enough to make the objects of such common ownership easily visible, as well as the struggle for their control.

The most important and wide-ranging issue separating Christians and pagans was the Christian insistence on worshiping one God at the expense of all others. The pagan objection to Christian exclusivism was actually a field of objections clustered about a common core, a theological center with implications far beyond the mathematics of monotheism. "Exclusivism" refers to more than simply the worship of the God of Israel and not the traditional deities of the Mediterranean basin. The term includes its practical manifestations as well, including elements of social and political exclusivism; it is here assumed that exclusivism had (and continues to have) consequences outside the realm of theology and that these are a valid subject of treatment in the literature of anti-Christian polemic. It is in this varied field with its consequences both philosophical and practical that this study focuses its attention, for the purpose of identifying those common elements for which pagans and Christians fought for control.

Another example shows how these elements illuminate the issue of exclusivism. The fact that the story of Jesus included ingredients not uncommon in pagan myths—a dying and rising deity, for instance, and the working of miracles—brought differing responses from pagans and Christians. To pagan critics, these areas of overlap undermined the Christian claim to exclusivism. If both Christ and Asclepius performed healing miracles, why must the worship of Christ preclude the worship of his rival? Besides, they argued, since Asclepius was clearly superior to Christ, the Christian demand for the exclusive worship of an "inferior deity" was ridiculous. Christians, on the other hand, while acknowledging the parallels between their religion and paganism, were forced to argue the reasons their deity was superior to pagan rivals. Such parallels accentuated, rather than submerged, the issue of Christian exclusivism. At the same time they identify for us an important point of contact between Christianity and paganism: the resonance, common to both sides of the debate, of a resurrected healer.

Such points of contact often produced friction. Perhaps nowhere was more heat produced than in the attempt of Christian intellectuals, especially from the turn of the third century onward, to position themselves as the legitimate heirs of Hellenistic culture and the Greek philosophical tradition. All three of the critics discussed in this study objected to this effort to one degree or another. While they insisted that the witness of both reason and antiquity argued against Christian monotheistic exclusivism, Christians used both to bolster their claim to possess the only true religion. This conflict formed a profound undercurrent to quite a large portion of the anti-Christian polemic, a current that more than occasionally broke the surface in explicit argument.

Nor were these issues restricted to the polemic literature. Christian exclusivism and the opposition to it were expressed in social, religious and philosophical contexts. These contexts changed dramatically during the period of our study, from the late second century to 363 CE. In the time of Celsus, Christianity was a struggling minority sect declaring its independence from Judaism, enduring persecution from both the populace and the state, and asserting itself as the rightful heir of both Judaism and Hellenistic culture. By the time of Julian, Christianity had become the imperially favored religion of the Roman Empire; within a generation afterwards, all pagan religious practices would be formally banned. It is to be expected that the anti-Christian polemic changed in important ways over the course of the nearly two centuries in question. For example, it is reasonable to expect a trend in the literature reflecting the growth of Christianity within society, specifically a movement from the criticism of Christian social exclusiveness to a protest against the dominance of Christian political power. Other trends are rhetorical in nature, reflecting changes in the critics' polemic strategy as the balance of religious and social power shifted in favor of their opponents. It is primarily these rhetorical trends, situated as they are in the shifting milieu of pagan-Christian relations, that constitute the subject of this book.

Our examination of pagan anti-Christian polemic has its origins in recent developments in patristic scholarship. The study of the growth of Christianity has shifted in recent years to the field of rhetoric, specifically the role of rhetoric in communicating Christian beliefs to the pagan world. Averil Cameron[3] in particular has traced the development of a "totalizing discourse" by which the Christian message became a complete worldview, a view that has been defined elsewhere as "a comprehensive interpretation of reality which subsumed or excluded other interpretations."[4] Using symbolic language, especially but not exclusively that of the Bible, the rhetoric of

the church became a totalizing discourse that attempted to eliminate ambiguity or dissent. The development of this discourse was
one of a number of factors to which the rise of Christianity can be
attributed.

But what of the pagan rhetoric against Christianity during the
same period? Thus far the study of the rhetorical dimensions of the
pagan-Christian conflict has focused on the Christian side, particularly the strategies by which Christian writers engaged their pagan
counterparts and their surrounding culture. This book initiates a
modest move toward the examination of the opposing pagan discourse. Specifically, this study addresses a series of questions: What
rhetorical strategies did the pagan polemicists employ against their
Christian opponents? Did they, like the Christians, create a "totalizing discourse" that radically excluded all Christian claims from
consideration? Or, given our brief discussion of the "common property" shared by the two sides, was such a discourse even possible?
Or were other strategies operative by which pagans attempted to
marginalize their opponents while acknowledging their often ambiguous boundaries?

The answers to these questions are necessarily complex. As we
have mentioned briefly, the pagan polemicists did not employ a
unified rhetorical strategy; in more than one instance contradictory
arguments are to be found between them. The fact that the period
under examination covers nearly two centuries complicates our task
by introducing a shifting field of inquiry. The Christianity of Julian's
day differed greatly from that of the time of Celsus; incidentally, the
failure to recognize this fact has hindered many an otherwise helpful comparison of Celsus' and Julian's polemic treatises. Their efforts
to marginalize the Christians as well as the strategies they used to
that end had to evolve, if for no other reason than that both Christianity and paganism underwent profound changes between the end
of the second century and the middle of the fourth.

Even over the course of the second century, before the introduction of Celsus' polemic, Christianity was being transformed from
an obscure offshoot of Judaism to a powerful religion in its own
right. The expansion of the new religion involved dramatic changes.
The process of self-definition vis-à-vis Judaism, for example, was at
least as old as the "council of Jerusalem" in the middle of the first
century. This process was accelerated by two Jewish revolts in 66–

70 and 132–135 CE, and by the middle of the second century Marcion was declaring Christianity independent in every way from its Jewish parent. On other fronts, the Montanist movement or "New Prophecy" raised serious questions regarding the continuation of divine revelation after the apostolic period. Throughout the empire the influence of gnosticism blossomed into the development of full-fledged schools of gnostic Christianity.

At the same time that these changes were taking place, the general public's knowledge of Christianity was growing. In the first decades of the second century, Pliny the Younger, governor of Bithynia-Pontus, appeared to know little or nothing about the strange religion whose adherents were being brought before his court. By the waning years of the same century, however, Christianity was gaining converts in large numbers, and the Latin apologist Tertullian could exclaim in about 197:

> Men cry that the city is filled with Christians; they are in the country, in the villages, on the islands; men and women, of every age, of every state and rank of life, are transferring to this group, and this they lament as if it were some personal injury.[5]

Whether or not Tertullian was exaggerating for effect is arguable. In any event, there seems to have been a notable difference between Christianity's relative obscurity in the early second century and the concern its growth had sparked at century's end. Such concern probably precipitated the writing of Celsus' anti-Christian treatise, the first of the three examined in this study. For this reason it is important to document the pagan understanding of, and opposition to, Christianity before the age of the polemicists.

With the exception of Nero's local action against Christians in Rome and a possible period of persecution under Domitian in the 90s CE, Christians enjoyed relative peace during the first century. Largely ignored by government officials, they were able to practice their religion in obscurity. By the early years of the second century, however, Christians were known well enough to be generally hated. For example, Tacitus' remark that Christians were viewed as *odium humani generis* was written fifty years after the Christians had been accused of setting great fire in Rome; it is likely that the historian was merely reflecting the prejudice of his own time. It is also likely, however, that the Christians' perceived hatred of humankind had indeed been sufficient for Nero to affix blame credibly. Their refusal to worship the gods would have been easily interpreted by outsiders as a tendency toward anarchy and even violence, especially since the gods were believed to be preservers of the peace.

Such popular opinion eventually led to the practice of informants turning Christians over to the local authorities. Perhaps representative of this practice in the early second century was the steady stream of Christians brought before the court of Pliny the Younger between 111 and 113 CE. Judging from his correspondence with the emperor Trajan on the matter, the governor himself seemed to know little or nothing about the people or the religion he was expected to judge. That a high Roman official, eighty years after the beginning of the Christian movement, should have to write to the emperor for guidance is indicative of the obscurity in which the religion had been able to operate up to this time. Now, however, the provincials of northern Asia Minor were bringing members of the troublesome group to the governor's attention and demanding action against them. Although Pliny executed some of these adherents to Christianity primarily for their obstinate behavior at his court, he also punished them for their refusal to conform to a basic standard of loyalty, that of offering incense to the images of the gods and of the emperor. It is quite possible that the scene was being repeated elsewhere in the empire.

An interesting statement of Pliny in the correspondence suggests that there may have been more to the accusations than meets the eye. According to his letter to the emperor, the very fact that he was conducting investigations of accused Christians "caused the charges to be more widespread and varied"; that is, more accusations surfaced when people heard that the governor was actively involved. One anonymous informant went so far as to publish a list of Christians as well as others who were merely suspected of being such, a list that Pliny apparently used to make a number of arrests. Many of the suspects denied the charge on the spot, although they admitted that they had once been adherents to Christianity.

> Others who were named by the informer said that they were Christians and then denied it; they were once but then ceased to be, some three years ago, some many years ago and some even twenty years ago.[6]

Why would the informants have made accusations against people who had forsaken Christianity and resumed worshiping the traditional gods two decades earlier (possibly as a result of Domitian's persecution)? Surely such people would not have fallen under immediate suspicion. It is possible that in these cases the accusation of "Christian" was employed as a "smear tactic," a tool of harassment against personal or political enemies. It is not difficult to imagine the anonymous informer including on his list the names of people he wanted to see brought before the authorities, whether they were Christians or not; if participation in Christianity tainted the victim's past, all the better. In any event, it is clear that in Asia Minor in the early second century the mere suspicion of being a Christian was grounds for accusation and harassment.

The contradiction in Trajan's reply to Pliny is curious. "They must not be sought out but if they are denounced and convicted they must be punished," adding that anonymous accusations have no place in criminal proceedings. How could it have been possible to reject anonymous accusations, yet act on them when they occurred? It is partially this lack of clarity that somewhat hampers our understanding of the motivations and procedures with regard to the persecutions of the second century.

What we can determine with at least some degree of certainty is that for the most part, persecutions in this period were not ordered by imperial edict; instead, they arose out of popular resentment toward the Christians. Although local magistrates and provincial governors allowed, encouraged, and sometimes instigated the persecutions, the anti-Christian action of the second century was frequently attributable to popular hatred. On the other hand, the anonymous list handed over to Pliny's court seems to have been produced only after official investigations had already begun; the governor did not specify what initial action had been taken by government officials. It may have been a similar series of anonymous accusations, possibly first introduced before a city council. It is also possible that the governor himself took the initiative. The former seems more likely, as Pliny wrote to the emperor for guidance only after the investigations were already underway. The driving force behind the harassment and execution of Christians appears to have originated in public resentment expressed to local officials.

During the decades following Pliny's governorship in 113, such accusations of a general nature developed into more specific propaganda. Stories circulated accusing Christians of various kinds of sexual immorality; charges of promiscuous intercourse and incest were commonly made against the Christians, charges that Christian apologists spent significant energy refuting. By mid-century, the rumors were coalescing into the often-repeated charges that indiscriminate sexual activity and cannibalism were being practiced at secret Christian gatherings. Cornelius Fronto (100–166 CE), the tutor of Marcus Aurelius, described the acts in which Christians were reportedly involved in lurid detail, denouncing in an oration the Christian movement and their supposedly bizarre practices in the decade of the 160s.

By the 170s, Christians were perceived as a serious threat to the public good. Perhaps partially in response to orations such as Fronto's, the period from about 150 to the late 170s witnessed a number of local mob actions against Christians, actions that may be characterized collectively as a widespread persecution. During this period Polycarp died at Smyrna, Sagaris in Laodicea, Carpus and Papylas at Pergamum. The summer of 180 saw groups of Christians executed at Madaura and Scilli in North Africa. Christians were being massacred in cities throughout the empire. Although the lynchings were supported and ultimately carried out by local government officials, the impetus seems to have come from the popular level. Not only had Christianity grown in numbers, it had grown in unpopularity to the point where groups of concerned citizens were motivated to take matters into their own hands.

The best-preserved example of a persecution initiated by the public and not by the legal system is that of the martyrs of Vienne and Lyons in Gaul, preserved by Eusebius in Book V of his *Ecclesiastical History*.[7] The outbreak seems to have been a cooperative effort between local magistrates, the people, and the provincial governor. The actual bringing of charges, however, was preceded by public harassments such as exclusion from public baths and assemblies. When the Christians finally appeared before the governor, the popular accusations of sexual immorality and cannibalism took center stage.

Curiously, this particular narrative lacks the inquisition scenes so common in other, later martyrologies; instead, the bulk of the narrative has to do with torture. Especially noteworthy is the absence of sacrifice to the emperor or the gods as an issue; either the Christians were not ordered to perform sacrifice or the writer thought it an irrelevant fact to report. The only involvement of the emperor was to order that Christians who were Roman citizens were to be beheaded instead of tortured, and that those who recanted were to be released. Evidence of the public nature of the episode appears in the fact that the governor dispatched a Roman citizen to the beasts and other tortures instead of beheading him, a violation of both the emperor's direct order and Roman custom. Such a violation is an important indicator of (local) official willingness to placate the crowd.

What dominates the actual charges in this narrative, both before and during the torture accounts, are the accusations of immorality described earlier. The tortures are introduced with charges reminiscent of Fronto's speech, accusations that the Christians are guilty of "feasts of Thyestes, and the incests of Oedipus." The last words on the lips of the Christians are denials of the charges of cannibalism, not their refusal to worship the gods. Declared one victim while being roasted alive, "Lo, this is to devour men, what you are doing. But as to us, we neither devour men nor commit any other evil."

Likewise the martyrdom of Polycarp in Smyrna seems to have been initiated by mob action, although there are some significant differences from the account of the martyrs of Gaul. The primary charge against Polycarp and the church at Smyrna was that of atheism, while during the proceedings at Lyons the accusations of immorality were more prevalent. The general tenor of the charges at Smyrna were made clear at Polycarp's sentencing: "This is the teacher of Asia, the father of the Christians, and the overthrower of our gods, he who has been teaching many not to sacrifice, or to worship the gods."

During the trial, the proconsul advised Polycarp to "swear by the genius of Caesar." This fact, however, need not indicate that the proceedings were conducted in accordance with any imperial decree, since Pliny had used a similar procedure even before consulting Trajan:

> Those who denied that they are or were Christians I have dismissed, when they invoked the gods (following my example) and made offering of frankincense and wine to your image (which I have commanded to be brought there together with the images of the gods for this purpose) and further-

more cursed Christ. It is said that those who are really Christians cannot
be forced to do any of these things.[8]

The death of Polycarp at Smyrna, like that of many Christians at
Lyons, was instigated by a mob with the active cooperation of the
authorities, with no decree having been promulgated by the emperor. Popular (and sometimes official, in the case of Fronto)
propaganda seems to have been the driving force in the rise of the
persecutions, propaganda that focused on the accusations of immorality and atheism.

The fact that several Christian apologists found it necessary to
refute these charges in the 170s illustrates the degree to which the
tales of immorality were taking hold in the popular imagination.
The three accusations made against the Christians at Lyons are also
found in the apology of Athenagoras as specific charges. "Three
things are alleged against us: atheism, Thyestean feasts, Oedipean
intercourse."[9] The accusations were repeated in the treatise of the
Christian apologist Theophilus, who in the decade of the 180s referred to the accusers as those who alleged

> that our wives are the common property of all and live in promiscuity,
> that we have intercourse with our own sisters, and—most godless and
> savage of all—that we partake of human flesh.[10]

The charges of immorality and atheism were widespread and deeply
felt. The public discourse through which pagans of all classes expressed their disgust with Christians was a "totalizing discourse"
of the first order. Enemies of the gods, of the state, and of the people,
Christians were considered unacceptable in every way, while the
propaganda and rumors served the purpose of marginalizing the
Christians as completely as possible. The boundaries between pagan and Christian were, at least on the surface, as clear as they would
ever be.

Then, for reasons unknown to us, the rumors seem to have
stopped. The charges of immorality virtually disappear from the
apologetic literature and the martyrologies. The public lynchings
ceased as well. Although persecution persisted through the turn of
the third century, Christians gained a measure of tolerance after the
savagery of the late 170s. The physician Galen could say that at

least some Christians "have attained a pitch not inferior to that of genuine philosophers."[11]

Summarizing the treatment of Christians throughout most of the second century, we observe that most of the opposition to Christianity was popular in nature; there would be no philosophical rejoinder until Celsus. Emperors provided little guidance, much less imperial decrees, for handling Christian offenders; Trajan's policy forbidding public officials to hunt down Christians seems to have been consistently followed. Informers, not police, were responsible for turning in Christians, and officials conducted trials only when the public initiated such action. Although Christians such as Polycarp were commanded to offer sacrifice to the emperor, this was meant only to separate the "obstinate" Christians from those who could be made to apostatize. Public opinion consisted largely of rumors about strange and immoral behavior in Christian gatherings. What else could explain the fact that they gathered in secret and refused to participate in respectable forms of worship? Although the general population undoubtedly knew some basic truths about Christians—that they refused to worship other gods, for example, or that their religion originated with a Jew named Jesus—pagan reaction was dominated by the belief that Christians were involved in bizarre and immoral behavior. There was little if any informed public opinion about Christianity during this period. The most important objections to Christianity were social, not philosophical. Systematic reflection by outsiders would not appear until Celsus near the turn of the third century, some time after the wave of public persecutions had crested.

Celsus' literary reply to Christianity was a symptom of the progress his opponents had made over the previous hundred years; when Christianity was little more than a secretive sect of Judaism, there had been no need for philosophical opposition. By the time Celsus and the other polemicists began their attack, however, their enemy had become a force to be reckoned with. The Christianity of the late second century and following was characterized by increasing intellectual sophistication, self-conscious separation from its Jewish parent, and a growing sense of mission. Perhaps most threatening of all to their pagan respondents, Christian thinkers were beginning to assert ownership of the cultural and intellectual property of their pagan opponents. This process would culminate with the Christians laying claim to the Greek and Roman classical past and, beginning with Constantine in the fourth century, to the empire itself. These claims would not go uncontested.

2

Celsus and the "Revolt Against the Community"

The late 170s was a time of crisis for Christianity; the last half of the decade had seen the most violent of the persecutions of the second century. But by decade's end, the public and sometimes illegal executions had ended; there would be no more mob-inspired persecutions for the next seventy years. Although rumors of Christian cannibalism and incest still circulated, they were no longer the staple of anti-Christian propaganda. The proliferation of Christian apologetic seems to have subsided as well. Some of the apologies had been addressed directly to Marcus Aurelius, the "philosopher-emperor," perhaps in the hope that an emperor with a philosophic cast of mind would be sympathetic to their pleas for toleration. His death in 180 may have removed any hope for such toleration, much less official recognition; as it happened, he had not at all been sympathetic to the Christians' plight. The only reference that the Christians received in his *Meditations* was an inconsequential note about the irrationality of their martyr instinct.

Even though the uglier rumors subsided, persecution continued. In place of the shouting mob, local magistrates conducted official proceedings under more carefully controlled conditions. At Scilli near Carthage in 180, for example, the trial of a dozen Christians was a relatively quiet affair. The proconsul Vigellius Saturninus engaged in patient debate with the accused, affirmed that "we too are a religious people," and gave the prisoners thirty days to change their minds.[1] Gone was the public spectacle only three years after its climax in Gaul; perhaps the excesses there had led the philosopher on the throne to impose moderation and legality upon the proceedings. Or perhaps the apologists' protests had reached the emperor after all.

Marcus Aurelius died in 180. His young son Commodus proved by all accounts to be a tyrant, and his assassination in 192 marked the end of the Antonine dynasty. An England-born soldier named Septimius Severus emerged as his successor after spending four years eliminating other contenders for the throne. The Severan dynasty which resulted continued until 235; during this time of prosperity the church enjoyed dramatic growth. Although sporadic persecutions continued through the reign of Severus until about 212, his successors over the next two decades extended unprecedented toleration to Christians and even entertained a few of them, including Origen, at court. Christians were rapidly becoming integrated into the larger society.

This integration resulted in a tension within the church: to what degree were Christians supposed to keep themselves pure, separated from the "pollution" of the world? Whatever the drawbacks of belonging to a small, persecuted minority, the boundaries had always been clear. Now these boundaries were becoming more ambiguous, and the resulting tension was manifesting itself in a number of ways. As early as the middle of the second century the Montanist movement, or New Prophecy as it is often called, was recalling Christians to a higher level of moral perfection. Although the movement indicates a divergence in ethical expectations within the church, more was at stake than issues of private morality. In North Africa, Tertullian felt compelled to argue against Christian participation in public amusements of any kind, such as the theater and games.

> We should have no connection with the things which we abjure, whether in deed or word, whether by looking on them or looking forward to them; but do we not abjure and rescind that baptismal pledge, when we cease to bear its testimony? Does it then remain to apply to the heathen themselves[?] Let them tell us, then, whether it is right in Christians to frequent the show. Why, the rejection of these amusements is the chief sign to them that a man has adopted the Christian faith.[2]

According to Tertullian, pagans understood that the renunciation of public amusements was a natural consequence of becoming a Christian. Nor was it only a matter of abstinence from the sexual or violent themes that were sometimes a part of these events. There were normally religious overtones as well, since the various games were commonly dedicated to particular deities. But with the increase in conversions to Christianity in the late second century, Christian integration into society included attendance at the games, although they continued to stay away from the more overt "idolatry" of the religious festivals. Whether this change is attributable to Christians' partial capitulation to pagan criticism or to other factors, the formerly small, isolated sect was starting to feel its way into the larger world. Tertullian's protest against Christian participation, as well as the fact that he became a Montanist himself later in life, is clear evidence that the time of Christian isolation had come to an end.

And yet the church as an institution had not emerged as a publicly acceptable entity by the year 200. The first large buildings dedicated to Christian worship were still several decades off. Christian Platonism was only now beginning to emerge in the writings of Clement of Alexandria, a philosophical project that would be continued by his successor Origen. At the turn of the third century the threat of persecution was still very real. Although individual Christians might decide to participate in some public events, the institutional church was still regarded as a dangerous and subversive "secret society."

Such was the precarious position in which Christians found themselves, and into which the first important literary attack, written by an otherwise unknown author named Celsus, was launched. His work was entitled Ἀληθὴς Λόγος (traditionally rendered *True Doctrine*) and is known only as it is quoted in Origen's refutation, *contra Celsum*. The *True Doctrine* was the first serious literary attack on Christianity; while several pagan authors of the second century had mentioned the Christians, Celsus' work was the first systematic treatise written against them.

Celsus' *True Doctrine* also represents an important transition in the substance of the accusations that pagans made against the church. Whereas earlier attacks had focused upon the crimes of immorality that Christians were alleged to have committed, Celsus' work marked the beginning of an era of philosophical attacks combined with reasoned refutation of the Christian scriptures. Of course, the critic did not abandon the practical issue of Christianity's offenses against society. To Celsus, Christians were a danger to the security of the state, a menace to orderly society, and an innovation that threatened traditional values. For the most part, however, Celsus was an informed polemicist, in general not relying on scandalous stories circulating about either Jews or Christians.[3] Instead, reporting from what appears to have been his own research, he concentrated his polemic largely on what he actually knew about the religion.

What was new, however, was a sustained philosophical and logical attack on the belief system, mythology, practices and sacred writings of Christianity. With this attack Celsus forged new weapons in the polemic war, weapons that later anti-Christian writers such as Porphyry and Julian would use with vigor. Not all of Celsus' objections were equally lasting, however; his arguments against Christian anti-social behavior, for example, were fading in the generation after Celsus. By the time Origen answered his polemic in about 248 CE, the arguments against Christian social exclusivism were largely irrelevant. Origen noted that some of his opponent's arguments had become obsolete in the interval between the writing of the *True Doctrine* and Origen's own apologetic reply. Celsus' philosophical arguments, however, would persist for centuries.[4] Celsus, then, represents a bridge between two styles of attack: the earlier objections based upon allegations of immorality and scandalous conduct, and the reasoned philosophical attack. The former were already losing their force by the time Celsus wrote the *True Doctrine*, while the latter was on the ascendancy.

To facilitate any investigation into the context of Celsus' work, a discussion of the date of his writing is in order. Such a discussion is necessary for two reasons. First, there is a broad consensus for the date of the *True Doctrine* that is based upon very slender evidence. For the last century and a half, the date has coalesced around the decade of the 170s, with a date of 178 cited most often. This consensus has remained remarkably firm, given the tenuous nature of the evidence. Second, and more important, it is necessary to establish the historical context for Celsus' polemic, a context that is vital for understanding his rhetorical strategy. Hence a brief excursus on the dating of Celsus is appropriate.

There are precisely three statements recorded in *contra Celsum* that scholars have used to date Celsus' *True Doctrine*.

1. Origen's statement that Celsus "has already been dead a long time,"[5] relative to the date of Origen's refutation in about 248.

2. Celsus' reference to the active persecution of Christians at the

time he wrote.[6]

3. Celsus' reference to "those who now reign over us."[7]

Let us examine the arguments for dating based on these statements. The first piece of evidence, that Celsus was dead "a long time" by 248, is subjective enough to allow for wide disagreement. We will set it aside for the moment. The second reference, alluding to persecutions occurring at the time of writing, is generally taken to coincide with the martyrdoms at Vienne and Lyons in 177 and the Scillitan martyrs of 180. Most scholars take the third clue, the reference to "those who now reign over us," as a literal reference to multiple rulers and so date Celsus' work to the coregency of Marcus Aurelius and his son Commodus in the years 177–180. Thus Chadwick assigns the *True Doctrine* "on balance" to the years 177–180 in the introduction to his translation of *contra Celsum*.[8] The great majority of scholars over the past century have agreed; a review of more recent church histories shows most commentators assuming a more exact date of 178.

However, there are reasons to advocate a later date for Celsus' polemic than the eighth decade of the second century, and especially later than the year 178. With regard to the third argument above, Celsus' use of the plural in reference to rulers need not refer to a joint imperium; he may have used the plural in a more general sense.[9] The rhetorical context of Celsus' statement regarding "those who now reign over us" supports such a general meaning, and because of the importance of this passage in discussions of Celsus' date it deserves to be quoted in full. This is especially true since references to the context have been notably absent in the literature.

> It is quite intolerable of you [Christians] to say that if those who now reign over us were persuaded by you and taken prisoner, you would persuade those who reign after them, and then others, if they too are taken prisoner, and others after them until, when all who are persuaded by you are taken prisoner, there will be a ruler who, being a sensible man and foreseeing what is happening, will utterly destroy you before you destroy him first.[10]

In the first place, if Celsus' first reference to a plurality of rulers is to be taken literally, it follows that he likewise meant for the subsequent "rulers" in the argument to reign together literally as well.

It seems unlikely, however, that Celsus would assume that joint reigns were to continue as a permanent feature of imperial rule in the future, especially given their rarity in the history of the empire before 177. In addition, although it has been argued[11] that the word "now" (νῦν) rules out a general interpretation of "rulers," it must be observed that Celsus' argument involves a hypothetical sequence of "rulers," the later ones contrasted with those who rule "now." The νῦν need not be taken to refer to actual conditions at the time of writing, since the word and its associated phrase are functioning within the framework of a hypothetical argument. Therefore the reference to a plurality of rulers need not refer to an actual coregency at the time of writing.[12]

With regard to argument 2 above, the widespread persecutions of the late second and early third centuries under Septimius Severus (193–211) are at least as likely a candidate for an era of active persecution as are those of 177–178. To this later period, for example, belong the *Martyrdom of Perpetua and Felicitas* as well as Tertullian's *Apology,* in which he protested the conduct of trials against Christians. Thus there is more than one possibility for assigning an "era" of persecutions to which Celsus refers.

Rejecting traditional interpretations of the evidence merely reopens the question. There are other available clues, however. More important than the individual arguments stated above is the fact, so frequently observed by students of *contra Celsum,* that Celsus was an informed critic of Christianity, not succumbing to the false charges of cannibalism and ritual intercourse so prevalent during the popular anti-Christian outbursts of the 170s. These charges were the central issues mentioned in the accounts of the martyrdoms at Vienne and Lyons and, along with the charge of atheism, were important issues in the Christian apologetic strategy of the same period.

Although the time around 178 marks the very height of these accusations, such charges are wholly absent from the *True Doctrine.* If Celsus was writing in 178, he would have been a rare exception indeed. However, is it not at least as reasonable to view Celsus as reflecting the more informed understanding of a later generation, and not writing as the sole enlightened exception during the apex of pagan misunderstanding? Celsus' reasoned responses to philosophical errors in Christian doctrine are quite out of step with the spirit of the 170s.

There are also some ancillary issues that may be addressed by recourse to a later date. For example, some have raised the question as to why Christian apologists did not answer Celsus' work immediately. If Celsus penned the *True Doctrine* in the late 170s, why was there not a Christian response until Origen's reply in 248, seventy years later?[13] Complicating this question is the fact that by the turn of the third century there were Christian minds more than adequate to meet the challenge that Celsus posed, apologists such as Tertullian of Carthage and Clement of Alexandria. Assigning a date for Celsus in the opening years of the third century, while perhaps not answering this question conclusively, at least closes the gap between challenge and response. In addition, there is no reason Origen's statement (argument 1 mentioned earlier) that Celsus "has already been dead a long time" would not allow a date around the turn of the third century, forty to fifty years before Origen's response in 248, as easily as it would allow a date in the 170s. Finally, it is also conceivable that Celsus' complaints in the *True Doctrine* against Christian proselytizing roughly correspond in time with a possible decree[14] of Septimius Severus in about 201 or 202 CE outlawing conversion to either Judaism or Christianity.

To be sure, a date near the turn of the third century is by no means secure. Our understanding of the dynamics of popular resentment for both the 170s and the following decades is certainly imperfect. The later date does not fully answer the question regarding the long response time of the church to Celsus' challenge. The link with Septimius Severus' decree, which is controverted as to authenticity, is tenuous. In addition, although we find most of the charges of immorality expressed in the last half of the decade of the 170s, they were not completely extinguished by the end of the second century; Tertullian was still defending the church against them in about 197.

On balance, though, it is at least as plausible to suggest a date of composition around the turn of the third century as it is to settle on the year 178. The failure of Celsus to capitalize upon the rumors so characteristic of popular resentment, combined with the fact that his criticisms appear to have been directed against a religious threat of increasing seriousness requiring a sustained intellectual response, bring us to break with scholarly consensus and offer a date of about 200 CE, plus or minus a decade, for the writing of the *True Doctrine*.

The dating of Celsus is not simply a matter of academic nicety. Placing his polemic (or any ancient writing, for that matter) into its historical context is normally essential for its interpretation. In this case, since the Christianity of the year 178 was in many ways different from that of around 200, a somewhat different opponent served as a target for pagan criticism. The passage of twenty years affected the objectives for which an anti-Christian treatise might have been written, as well as the specific strategies this particular critic used to launch his attack. These strategies are especially important to us as we compare Celsus to his successors.

Celsus' criticism was not only the first treatise to be written against Christianity, it represents the first known use of consciously Platonic categories to refute various aspects of Christian doctrine and mythology. At the same time, as philosophically oriented as parts of Celsus' criticism were, the social aspects of Christianity constituted a significant element of his argument. According to Origen, the issue of Christian social exclusivism constituted the opening salvo of the *True Doctrine.*

> Celsus' first main point in his desire to attack Christianity is that the Christians secretly make associations with one another contrary to the laws, because societies which are public are allowed by the laws, but secret societies are illegal. . . . After this he says that Christians perform their rites and teach their doctrines in secret, and they do this with good reason to escape the death penalty that hangs over them.[15]

Furthermore, according to Celsus, Christians were still worshiping in private homes and were not attending the festivals dedicated to the gods. Their social exclusivism was not, however, simply a matter of social passivity. Christians did not carry on their proselytizing activities in the normal venues for philosophical discussion; instead, Christian evangelists worked from house to house, preaching to children, women and slaves. Although Christians had begun to press the boundaries between church and society, they were far from being fully integrated into that society.

Celsus' observation that Christians worshiped in secret was not merely a note on their meeting habits; it was a statement that Christianity was outlawed and should continue as such. "Secret societies" of various types were indeed illegal, as Pliny's correspondence to Trajan indicates, in which it was related that the emperor banned all such associations or *hetaeria*. While some writers have objected that Christian gatherings were not actually illegal at the time Celsus wrote, his reference to the death penalty is fairly clear; Origen's failure to contradict the statement adds weight to Celsus' observation. On the other hand, it is not the illegality of Christian assembly that is Celsus' main thrust here, although it may well have been illegal at the time, but the fact that Christians were meeting in secret at all. Celsus' complaint against "secret associations" implies that Christians were a group of subversives that were a threat to societal order.

Apparently, the fact that a number of Christians were attending some public functions by this time was insufficient to satisfy Celsus that they were truly on their way to becoming part of the larger culture. To be an acceptable member of society meant participating in the cults of the gods who kept society peaceful and stable. Rejection of the gods was, by definition, a rejection of society. But there was more to Celsus' admoniton than a desire for Christians to become more fully integrated into society; there were theological stakes as well.

> This is what [Celsus] says: God is surely common to all men. He is both good and in need of nothing, and without envy. What, then, prevents people particularly devoted to [him] from partaking of the public feasts? . . . This is what he says: If these idols are nothing, why is it terrible to take part in the high festival? And if they are daemons of some sort, obviously these too belong to God, and we ought to believe them and sacrifice to them according to the laws, and pray to them that they may be kindly disposed.[16]

The theological thrust of Celsus' argument allows us a glimpse into the genesis of a debate between pagans and Christians concerning the nature of God. In the immediate context this debate touched upon two theological subpoints, namely God's universality and impassibility. The first point, that "God is surely common to all men," was a direct attack upon Christian exclusivism, implying that the supreme deity could not be the possession of a single group, or even of a single nation. God was "common to all," that is, accessible to people of all nations, whether pagan, Jew or Christian. In addition, Celsus' statement regarding the daemons that "these too belong to God" implied that all religious activity honored the supreme deity, whether intended directly for that deity or indirectly through the lesser gods. Since this was the case, Christians should have nothing to fear from participating in pagan worship, no matter what nation, pantheon, or religious tradition was involved. Since Christians claimed to worship the supreme deity, pagan religious activities ought to be a perfectly acceptable means of doing so.

Here, then, are the social implications of the theological issue: if God is supreme and thus κοινός to all, then all people have the same access to this deity through the intermediary agency of the gods. Celsus' objection that God was universal or "common" was theological in nature, but social in its application. It was therefore unreasonable for Christians to separate themselves socially and religiously—in short, to behave in a socially exclusive manner. Here we glimpse Celsus' linkage between Christian social and theological exclusivism, as well as the ways in which the objections to both kinds interact with each other in the course of the polemic.

Celsus' second theological argument in the passage quoted above begins with divine impassibility: if the supreme God can experience neither need nor envy, how can the worship of the daemons offend him? According to Celsus, Christian monotheism should not stand in the way of participating in the feasts. The critic presented an apparently insoluble dilemma: either the daemons were non-existent, in which case the feasts were harmless, or they belonged to the supreme God, in which case they were worthy of worship. Either way, Christian worship of the gods could not offend a God incapable of jealousy. What is missing from Celsus' logic, of course, is the third option argued elsewhere by Origen: that the daemons did indeed exist, but that they were in fact evil and not worthy of worship at all. First found in Justin Martyr, the Christian apologist of the middle of the second century, this early Christian argument asserted that the Greek and Roman gods were in reality "wicked and impious demons."

Celsus' argument regarding the gods was, of course, based on the criticism that Christians were abstaining from public festivals dedicated to the gods. But what we are witnessing in the exchange from Justin to Celsus to Origen was more than a battle over the status of Christian social participation; it was ultimately a conflict over the nature of God. In Celsus' context the conflict was twofold, as it touched upon both the status of subordinate beings and the impassibility of God. First, as we mentioned in the first chapter, the existence of the gods was not a matter of debate. Christians accepted their reality, provided that they were to be seen as nothing more than wicked spirits; pagans and Christians alike accepted the fact of a supernatural realm filled with spiritual beings in direct contact with humanity and the physical world. Second, Celsus complained that jealousy on the part of the Christians' God violated the generally held idea that God was incapable of emotion. This complaint constituted a powerful argument for the very reason that the Christians believed it too; divine impassibility was not a doctrine that Christians were inclined to reject. Celsus' polemic against Christian social exclusivism reveals important points of contact between the pagan and Christian theological universes, connections that would accompany Christianity on its march toward dominance over the Late Antique world.

A final objection of Celsus that dealt with the social aspects of Christian exclusivism concerned proselytizing. In an extended quotation preserved by Origen, Celsus complained harshly against the Christian practice of using the promises of Christianity to lure children away from their families. Such a charge of inciting children to leave home and despise their parents would have been extremely serious, reminiscent of the charge leveled at Socrates that he was corrupting the youth of Athens. The structure of the Roman family would have added further gravity to Celsus' charges. The father possessed absolute authority in the home, and an invitation to despise the father and to rebel against his authority would have been viewed as a serious breach of social norms. It may be conjectured that the charge of inciting familial rebellion also served as a rhetorical parallel to the other accusations of rebellion so frequently made against the Christians and which are prominent in Celsus' treatise. Just as Christians were rebels from approved religions, from governmental authority, and from established tradition, they were also rebels against that most ancient of social structures, the family.

Thus far we have examined several dimensions of Celsus' objection to Christian social exclusivism, such as the secrecy of Christian worship, the failure of Christians to attend public events, and the undermining of pagan homes in order to make converts. How true were these objections? Were his characterizations based on the actual condition of the church at the time? Although this is a study of Celsus' rhetoric and not primarily of Christian social history, comparing his objections to what we know of the historical situation will assist us in evaluating the rhetoric.

We have argued previously that at the time Celsus wrote the *True Doctrine,* around the turn of the third century, Christianity was in the middle of a decades-long process of emerging from relative social isolation into the mainstream of Græco-Roman society. Tertullian's complaint against Christians who attended public events appeared about this time. The number of converts was increasing, and not only from the lower classes. Although the church was far from attaining social acceptability, it was no longer huddled in the dark corners of society. Nor was this only the case at the end of the second century. Even in the earlier account of the Gallic martyrdoms of 178, pagan persecutors excluded Christians from baths, markets and other public gathering places before actually excercising violence against them. Therefore Christians were not withdrawn completely from society; on the contrary, pagans sometimes imposed social isolation upon them as a prelude to persecution. This being the case, Celsus' characterization of Christians as radically isolated and anti-social sounds one-sided at least. His presentation is mildly anachronistic, perhaps several decades too late to be fully accurate, yet containing just enough truth to avoid sounding completely implausible. In short, considering the situation of the church at the time, Celsus' objection to Christian social exclusivism has the ring of propaganda to it.[17]

Why would Celsus have misrepresented the church in this manner? Why, during the very era that Christians were struggling with the issues involved in integrating themselves into the larger society, did Celsus paint a picture of radical social withdrawal? There are several good reasons, not least of all the fact that the critic was engaged in polemic discourse, not impartial reporting. Pagans had successfully characterized the Christians as "haters of humanity" for as much as a century by this time, and there was no reason to stop using the familiar rhetoric now. Besides, the fact that Christianity still had neither official nor popular sanction made it as suspect as ever to many. In addition, the church had not yet reached the status it would enjoy by the middle of the third century, a status which would include the amassing of substantial wealth, the construction of church buildings, and a sustained intellectual tradition. Celsus' rhetoric of Christian separatism was still partially true; after all, half-truths make the best propaganda.

There may have been another reason for Celsus to engage in an overstatement of Christian social exclusivism, a reason that will require some discussion of a possible change in official policy toward the Christians. There was a substantial difference between the public expression of anti-Christian fury in 177–8 which included the illegal execution of Roman citizens and the controlled, legal prosecution of Christians at the court at Scilli in 180. It is possible that there was a formal move on the part of the government to take control of anti-Christian action during this period. As much of a threat as Christians posed to order, the threat of unrestrained public passion was just as great, even if directed against a public enemy. Perhaps the empire, anxious to preserve order, moved to take control of all anti-Christian action; persecutions would now be initiated only by imperial order and by local magistrates, not by the public. Perhaps Marcus Aurelius made the decision before embarking on a two-year campaign against the Germans on the Danube in 178. Such a scenario, if correct, means that the state's acquisition of the prerogative of persecuting Christians—it had always possessed the actual power, as Nero had demonstrated a century earlier, but had rarely exercised it—removed from the populace the right to initiate violence against the church. Whether or not an actual decree to this effect can ever be demonstrated, the martyrdoms in Gaul were the last to occur at the instigation of a mob for many decades. The era of public persecutions had for all practical purposes ended.

It is suggested that the establishment of state control over the right to persecute enabled the church to exert a presence in society previously impossible because of public pressure. Although the prosecution of Christians still occurred, such action was now largely in the hands of the government. As it happened, most local officials initiated persecution only when ordered by imperial edict, such as the persecution of Decius in the middle of the third century, or when Christians engaged in visible demonstrations of disloyalty to the state or other disruptive activities. Otherwise, Christians were by and large left alone. The church was free to determine its own course with regard to social integration, a process that was well underway by the year 200.

By the time Celsus wrote the *True Doctrine*, the church was beginning to emerge into the mainstream of pagan society. This emergence, itself a cause of friction and division within the church, was now a cause of alarm for pagans, and was perhaps the reason Celsus took up the challenge of refuting Christianity in the first place. His characterization of his opponents as a small isolationist sect was in large part a reaction against the growth of the church and its social integration, and as such was a propagandistic half-truth; not only would such a description be false by the time Origen replied to the critique several decades later, it was not wholly true in Celsus' own day. Since the critic feared the potential for harm that Christianity represented to Roman society, he was concerned to preserve that society from the religion's influence. Seeing the cultural threat, Celsus' task was to put the genie back into the bottle.

His rhetorical solution was thus a totalizing discourse of radical exclusion. According to Celsus, Christian social exclusivism, a consequence of exclusive monotheism, marked the Christians off as enemies of society, the state, and the family. Nowhere in this aspect of the polemic did Celsus consciously yield that there might be areas of overlap between Christianity and paganism; Christianity was completely "other," an outside threat diametrically opposed to the social order. However, Celsus' attempt to reinforce the barriers between Christian and pagan was occurring at the very time that Christians in the real world were succesfully tearing them down.

Thus far we have primarily examined Celsus' criticism of Christian social exclusivism. More prominent in the *True Doctrine* as a rhetorical device, however, is his use of Judaism as a weapon against the Christians. There are several reasons for examining such a use of Judaism in the polemic. In the first place, the literature itself demands such an examination; the appearance of Jews and Judaism is not an inconsequential element in the anti-Christian writings. Since even a cursory reading of Celsus, Porphyry and Julian reveals that Judaism dominates the discourse to an overwhelming degree, it is surprising that most scholarship concerning our three critics gives short shrift to the Jewish issue.[18] The relationship of Christianity to Judaism was not only of great theological concern to Christian interpreters of the Hebrew Bible, it was a primary focus of pagan observers of Christianity.

Second, Christianity and Judaism represented the two exclusive universalisms of the Roman Empire. In this respect they stood side by side as targets of pagan criticism, giving us insight into how this common element influenced the polemic. For example, was Judaism more acceptable to the critics than Christianity? Or were both religions equally criticized? How did the two religions fare in the anti-Christian polemic when compared to each other? The treatment of Judaism and Christianity allows us to detect the specific rhetorical strategies by which the pagan critics differentiated, or failed to differentiate, the two.

These strategies differed among our polemicists, leading to the final reason the examination of the Jewish factor is important for this book. The rhetorical treatment of the Jews compared to that of the Christians provides an important measuring device for studying changes in the polemic strategies employed over the period covered in this study, particularly between Celsus and Julian. These changes are dependent in some degree upon differences in historical context, and it is to the situation at the turn of the third century that we now turn.

During the time of Celsus, the church was still struggling with its identity with respect to Judaism. This internal conflict began as early as the Council of Jerusalem, recorded in Acts 15 and which resolved the status of Gentile converts with respect to Torah. The practical issues of circumcision and ethics are reflected in the New Testament, particularly in the epistle of Paul to the Galatians and the epistle of James. By the middle of the second century, Marcion asserted not only that the Hebrew Bible and the New Testament were incompatible, but that the Gods presented in each Testament were completely different from each other. According to Marcion, the jealous, vengeful God of the Jews was not to be confused with the loving Father of Jesus Christ. Although the larger catholic church condemned Marcion, his movement and the issues that brought it into being forced the church to grapple significantly with its relationship to Judaism and to its Jewish origins.

There is also some evidence that the struggle was not entirely internal to the church, but that Christians and Jews were engaged in disputation during the early church period. Debate seems to have been joined early over issues such as circumcision, Sabbath observance, and the proper interpretation of the scriptures. The surviving disputation literature, which extends into the Middle Ages, is entirely of Christian origin. As a result the genre has come under particular scrutiny in recent years, particularly as it came to serve an anti-Jewish agenda.[19] Justin's *Dialogue with Trypho,* written in the middle of the second century, is in many ways prototypical of later (and probably fictional) "dialogues." However, Justin's *Dialogue* does bear some marks of authenticity, such as the statement that the Jew Trypho was a refugee from the Bar Cochba revolt. In addition, Trypho did not convert to Christianity at the end of the *Dialogue,* while the baptism of Jewish opponents is a trademark of later works. In the second century at least, if Justin's account is in any way typical of the situation, there was some level of active discussion between Jews and Christians.[20]

Celsus claimed to be a witness to these disputations. Basing his polemic for the most part not upon rumor but on observation and investigation, the critic understood what the two religious groups had in common: one God, the Bible of the Jews, and the refusal to recognize the validity of pagan religions. He also recognized what divided them, such as Torah observance and the status of Jesus. Whether or not Celsus' characterization of these "dialogues" has any basis in events he actually witnessed, his description gives us at least his own impression of Jewish-Christian argument.

> After this [Celsus] continues as usual by laughing at the race of Jews and Christians, comparing them all to a cluster of bats or ants coming out of a nest, or frogs holding council round a marsh, or worms assembling in some filthy corner, disagreeing with one another about which of them are the worse sinners.[21]

At this juncture Celsus is merely engaging in name-calling. What is important to note at the outset, however, is his equal rhetorical treatment of Jews and Christians, a trend that continues throughout the *True Doctrine.* This treatment retains particular importance as we compare Celsus' polemic with that of his successors.

First, however, it is necessary to discuss in general terms some of the issues involved in the use of Judaism in the pagan anti-Christian literature. The fact that Christianity had its origins in Judaism provided a large amount of polemic material for pagan critics. As we have seen briefly, Celsus exploited long-standing disagreements between Jews and Christians in order to characterize both as engaging in meaningless and self-defeating argument.

However, just as important as the polemicists' use of Judaism was how they used it. For the critics, Judaism was useful as a "weapon" against their Christian opponents, a two-edged sword that could be wielded in both directions. In the first place, there had been a long history of pagan-Jewish antagonism during the Hellenistic period, culminating in two Jewish revolts against Roman rule in 66–70 and 132–135 CE. Much of this hostility seems to have been transferred to the Christians, especially over the course of the second century, for many of the same reasons. Christians, like Jews, were hostile to "idolatry" and thus were viewed as hostile to society and as a threat to the state. It has been noted that the composition of pagan anti-Jewish polemic ceased altogether in the middle of the second century,[22] possibly coinciding with the growth of Christianity during this period.

However, particularly in the case of Celsus, there was more than a simple transference of old anti-Jewish arguments to the Christians. The pagan field of vision did not merely shift from one object to the next. On the contrary, although anti-Jewish polemic literature *per se* ceased, pagans continued to utilize anti-Jewish argument in their criticism of Christianity; they linked Christians with Jews in a form of "guilt by association." Whenever the Jews came under criticism in anti-Christian polemic, it was argued further that the Christians were equally objectionable because of their Jewish origins. Similarly, when a particular aspect of Christianity came under pagan attack, the fact that that characteristic existed also in Judaism made the criticism more effective. Thus we observe the persistence of anti-Jewish polemic, only for a different purpose—as a weapon against the Christians.

The second way in which pagan critics used Judaism against their Christian opponents was to contrast Christian belief or practice with something positive the critic saw in Judaism. Julian was the most proficient practitioner of this tactic. Specifically, the ceremonial requirements of Jewish law and particularly the biblical requirement for blood sacrifices were examples of what was best in Judaism that the Christians left behind. However, a pagan critic's acceptance of a particular Jewish belief or practice was not necessary for this tactic to be effective. Regardless of whether or not any-thing specific in Judaism was worthy of praise, Christians were culpable for abandoning their religious heritage. The very act of disregarding a traditional belief, no matter how strange or objectionable it might have seemed to the pagan polemicist, was itself an act of sacrilege.

It is true that the criticism of Judaism in the polemic was only a secondary goal, since Christianity was the real target. However, it is equally important to understand that the pagan critics differed from one another in their use of Judaism against the Christians. These differences are important. As we observe the development of the use of Judaism in the anti-Christian literature, we witness substantial changes from Celsus to Julian. Celsus' treatment of the Jews was overwhelmingly negative, while Julian favored the Jews both in his anti-Christian literature and in his political actions. This difference in the treatment of Judaism provides an important indication of the shift in the rhetorical treatment of Christianity between the turn of the third century and the time of the last pagan emperor in 362–363.

A substantial portion of Celsus' anti-Christian polemic is anti-Jewish; his strategy of associating his opponents with a generally despised religious and ethnic minority constitutes an important element of the overall attack. Thus nearly his entire treatment of Judaism in the *True Doctrine* uses the tactic of "guilt by association," the first of the two strategies described above. When, for example, he refers to Christian teaching as "originally barbarian,"[23] he hopes to demonstrate by association that Christianity is as "barbaric" as Judaism. Like parent, so to speak, like child. By adding that "the Greeks are better able to judge the value of what the barbarians have discovered," Celsus places the construct of the "civilized" Greeks in the rhetorical position of power, thus appropriating the cultural authority to evaluate both Christianity and Judaism.

The inferiority of both Jewish and Christian origins remains a prominent theme throughout the *True Doctrine*, particularly in the context of Celsus' attack on the personalities of Moses and Jesus. While the polemicist on more than one occasion refers to Moses as a "sorcerer," he also applies the same epithet to Jesus. At one point he uses the term with reference to the Christians themselves. Moses and Jesus thus belonged to the same class of undesirables, while their followers share their despised status. Celsus also applies other associations between Moses and Jesus and their followers; prominent throughout his polemic are the recurring themes of deceiver and deceived, charlatans leading the illiterate and uncultured, sorcerer and followers. In addition, the Jews, according to Celsus, were originally renegades from Egypt, while Christians were likewise renegades from Judaism.

> In his next remarks Celsus imagines that the Jews were Egyptian by race, and left Egypt after revolting against the Egyptian community and despising the religious customs of Egypt. He says that what they did to the Egyptians they suffered in turn through those who followed Jesus and believed him to be the Christ; in both instances a revolt against the community led to the introduction of new ideas.[24]

According to Celsus, Jews and Christians shared the same group characteristics and therefore deserved to be condemned together, whether with respect to their origins or in the present.

Celsus also criticized the Bible, particularly the Hebrew Scriptures, in an effort to attack the myths and doctrines of both Jews and Christians. We have previously noted Celsus' objection to God's jealousy as part of an attack on Christian social exclusivism; he also ridiculed similar presentations of God in the scriptures as indicating that God was a vindictive and arbitrary deity. In addition, according to Celsus, the Hebrew Bible was filled with immoral behavior on the part of God's people, while God himself was weak, since he was unable to control Adam and Eve in the Garden of Eden. In these and many other ways, the polemicist presented Jewish and Christian beliefs and writings as irrational and immoral.

In addition to these direct criticisms of Judaism are what may be considered indirect efforts to marginalize the Jews rhetorically. Thematic in Celsus' writing—as well as the inspiration for the title of his treatise—is a "true doctrine" held by the wisest of nations and individuals, a teaching that incorporated the most ancient religious myths and philosophical wisdom. Significantly, according to Origen, Celsus did not include the Jews among the "wisest nations" that possessed this doctrine, nor did he include Moses in his list of the wisest men. Origen's response makes it clear that he noticed the omission in his own text of the *True Doctrine*.

Thinking that between many of the nations there is an affinity in that they
hold the same doctrine, Celsus names all the nations which he supposes
to have held this doctrine originally. But for some unknown reason he
misrepresents the Jews alone, and does not include their race in the list
with the others. . . . And he would not speak of the Jews as being a very
wise nation on a par with the Egyptians, Assyrians, Indians, Persians,
Odrysians, Samothracians, and Eleusinians.[25]

The "unknown reason" to which Origen refers is obvious enough
from what we know of Celsus' strategy. Associating the Christians
with the Jews was central to Celsus' polemic project; his strategy
throughout the *True Doctrine* was to represent the Jews as a con-
temptible people with questionable origins and an irrational religion
in order to attack the Christians, their spiritual offspring. Including
the Jews and Moses in a discussion of the wisest nations and people
would have seriously undermined this strategy.

One final aspect of Celsus' rhetoric of Judaism deserves additional examination. We have summarized his use of the Jews and
Judaism to provide a polemic association with his real opponent,
the Christians. There is, however, a lengthy section of the *True Doctrine* that reveals an interesting aspect of his strategy. As well-stocked
as Celsus' polemic arsenal was, there seems to have been a source of
anti-Christian material that he consciously neglected to employ, that
of Jewish anti-Christian argument.

We know from Justin's *Dialogue with Trypho* that there were differences of opinion between Jews and Christians regarding the
interpretation of certain passages of the Hebrew Bible, particularly
those that Christians held to be messianic in reference. In addition
to providing the Christian interpretation of these passages, Justin's
work provides several specific instances of Jewish refutation. One
of the more well-known christological interpretations that Justin
mentions is that of Isaiah 7:14, which Christians used to refer to the
virgin birth of Christ. Jews had apparently argued against the Christian translation of the Hebrew העלמה as "the virgin." In the *Dialogue*
Justin tells his Jewish opponent that

you and your teachers venture to affirm that in the prophecy of Isaiah it is
not said, "Behold, the virgin shall conceive," but, "Behold, the young
woman shall conceive, and bear a son". . . I shall endeavor to discuss shortly

this point in opposition to you. . . .[26]

Thus the argument was current as early as the middle of the second century and probably available to Celsus. Given the relatively large amount of space Celsus seems to have used in the *True Doctrine* to refute the idea of a virgin birth,[27] the straightforward argument that Christians were misinterpreting this passage of scripture is curiously absent from the polemic. That the omission was not a textual accident is shown by the fact that Origen, presumably working with the full text of Celsus' treatise, felt compelled to supply the argument for his opponent!

The same observations can be made for other Christian interpretations of the Hebrew Bible. These interpretations included the use of the first person plural in the Genesis account of creation ("Let us make man in our image, in our likeness. . ."), which Justin used to argue that God the Father was speaking to the preincarnate Christ.[28] Justin also indicated that the opening line of Psalm 110, "The Lord said to my Lord"—interpreted messianically in Acts 2:34— was interpreted by Jews to mean that God was speaking to King Hezekiah.[29]

There are two possible explanations for the fact that Celsus did not employ existing Jewish arguments against Christian interpretations of prophecy. In the first place, it is quite possible that Celsus was unaware of these Jewish objections. Such unawareness would be understandable. His understanding of his opponent, while certainly more complete than any of the other pagan writers who mentioned Christianity in the first two centuries, was of course imperfect. At one point in his polemic, however, Celsus used a tale known from the Talmud that Jesus was the illegitimate son of Mary and a Roman soldier named Pantera,[30] demonstrating that Celsus had access to at least this element of Jewish anti-Christian material. More important is the fact that Celsus himself claims to have been acquainted with a particular Jewish-Christian dialogue, no longer extant, entitled *The Discussion Between Jason and Papiscus*. Thus Celsus was not wholly ignorant of Jewish arguments against Christianity.

The second reason Celsus may not have used Jewish sources is that he did not wish to do so. While Celsus was indeed familiar with at least some Jewish arguments against Christianity, it would not have served his rhetorical purpose to use them. Whether his non-use of Jewish arguments represents a deliberate suppression on Celsus' part or merely a selective choosing of sources for anti-Christian argumentation is largely irrelevant. Celsus presumably had available to him the Jewish side of the argument through Justin's *Dialogue with Trypho,* yet these arguments are completely absent from his polemic. While Justin's work spent a great deal of energy presenting the Christian interpretation of prophecy as well as various Jewish arguments against these interpretations, Celsus omitted altogether these potentially useful sources of anti-Christian material. Such an omission from the *True Doctrine* was entirely compatible with his rhetorical strategy of associating, not distinguishing, Christianity and Judaism.

Evidence for this omission appears in two sections of *contra Celsum.* The first section comprises a substantial portion of the *True Doctrine* and is composed of Celsus offering his arguments through the literary figure of a Jew. This device is used two ways. In Book 1 of *contra Celsum* the Jew argues directly with Jesus,[31] while in the entirety of Book 2 he argues with a Jew who has become a Christian.[32] Most of the time in this section, Celsus' use of the Jew as a mouthpiece against the Christians is curious in that he presents a number of arguments ill-suited for a Jew to make. He remarks to Jesus, for example, that there is nothing special about Jesus' blood, since it was not "Ichor such as flows in the veins of the blessed gods." The Jew proceeds to compare the story of Jesus' virgin birth to the divine births of Perseus, Amphion, Aeacus and Minos, although he hastens to add parenthetically that he does not believe these myths either. To refute the claim of Jesus' resurrection the Jew produces a lengthy list of characters from Greek history and mythology who claimed to have risen from the dead. That the arguments are clearly non-Jewish is exemplified by his curious statement that since Jesus was a practicing Jew he could not have been the son of God. Had Celsus at any time been inclined to use anti-Christian arguments from Jewish sources, it would have been in this section; what he puts in the mouth of the Jewish figure, however, is extremely odd, especially as the statements are at times anti-Jewish.

The second section of *contra Celsum* that suggests evidence for a deliberate omission of Jewish argument consists of a rather straightforward complaint against the exclusivism of Jewish prophecy, a section that constitutes a substantial portion of Book 7 of Origen's refutation. Here Celsus attacks both the prophetic literary genre of the Hebrew Bible and what he describes as contemporary oral prophetic utterances. While his subject is both predictive prophecy and the prophecy of proclamation, Celsus' primary purpose is to criticize Christian reliance on predictive prophecies from the Hebrew Bible. Four such specific arguments may be detected in this section: the argument against the exclusivism of Jewish prophecy, especially in light of "approved" oracles such as that of Apollo at Delphi; a mockery of the style of oral prophecy that Celsus alleges was common in the eastern Mediterranean; a series of arguments against anti-philosophical readings of prophecy that Christians used to substantiate their claims that Jesus was the predicted Messiah; and the argument that the teachings of Moses and Jesus contradict each other, thus invalidating one or both. It is an appropriate time in the *True Doctrine* for Celsus to introduce Jewish refutations of Christian messianic interpretations of prophecy. This is particularly the case in *contra Celsum* 7.12–15, in which he attacks irrational Christian interpretations of predictive prophecy. Such Jewish refutations are, however, completely absent. Nor does the fragmentary state of Celsus' text explain their absence; Origen, with the text of the *True Doctrine* before him, also notes the lack.[33]

While Origen speculated that Celsus' omission was due to his inability to refute the strength of predictive prophecies about Christ, another explanation is more likely. Celsus' use of Judaism throughout the *True Doctrine* was almost entirely a strategy of Christian "guilt by association," not a strategy of contrast with Judaism. Had he used Jewish arguments to refute Christian interpretations of scripture, he would have run the risk of giving Judaism favorable treatment. Even when a Jewish interpretation would have bolstered his anti-Christian argument considerably, Celsus neglected it. This neglect is particularly significant since Celsus had access to other Jewish arguments against Christianity,[34] as indicated by his use of the Pantera story and by his knowledge of written Jewish-Christian dialogue. Since he apparently researched Jewish arguments against Christianity in preparation for writing his polemic treatise, he had an opportunity to use other Jewish counterarguments to the Christian use of the Hebrew Bible.

Thus Celsus' failure to capitalize upon the existence of Jewish anti-Christian argumentation was related to his rhetorical strategy with respect to Judaism; the polemicist was more concerned to associate than to distinguish Christianity and Judaism. Pointing out differences between Jewish and Christian interpretations of the same prophetic passages would have undermined his rhetorical strategy of association; giving credence to the Jewish interpretations of scripture over the Christian ones would have worked against this strategy as well. Although such information was available to him he seems to have deliberately ignored it in order to preserve his more important and long-term goal, namely to discredit the Christians entirely by discrediting the religious tradition from which they originated.

Thus far, we can safely characterize Celsus' rhetorical strategy as a totalizing discourse, one that allowed no legitimacy to his opponents. So important was this strategy that he was even willing to ignore significant sources of anti-Christian argument when the use of those sources would have come into conflict with his larger rhetorical purpose. Celsus admitted no common ground between paganism and Christianity; although we have detected in his theological arguments several elements of common belief, these elements are incidental to, not part of, his polemic approach.

Celsus' strategy emerged within a historical context in which Christianity was making significant progress in its integration with society, an integration that Tertullian was protesting even while Celsus was denying its existence. To be sure, the Christian rejection of the gods would prove an enduring boundary, even if aspects of Christianity had some elements in common with pagan mythology, as we will see in the next chapter. One aspect of Christian integration that would become ever more controversial, however, was the attempt on the part of Christians from the time of Justin, decades before the writing of the *True Doctrine*, to appropriate Hellenistic philosophy. What, then, would be the Celsus' treatment of his opponents from a philosophical perspective? How would Celsus, a Platonist, counter the Christian tendency to employ Plato as an ally of their own?

3

Celsus, Plato, and the Gods

One of the observations frequently made in the study of early Christianity is the wealth of syncretism between Christianity and pagan religion and culture. Naturally, Christianity "borrowed" greatly from its Greek and Roman surroundings, not a surprising observation given their common religious genetics. The ubiquitous presence of the gods gradually metamorphosed into the shrines of the saints; aspects of pagan religious art and the prophetic tradition were transformed for Christian use.[1] Only a short step was required, for example, for the third-century Egyptians who compiled the Hermetic writings (or, more accurately, their intellectual successors) to embrace Christianity:

> The Hermetist, when he became a Christian, would not have so very much to unlearn. . . . He had been accustomed to aspire towards union with God, and to hold that "to hate one's body" is the first step on the way to the fulfilment of that aspiration; and when we come upon him, a little later on, transformed into a Christian hermit in the Egyptian desert, we find that he is still of the same opinion.[2]

While most scholars observe the influence of paganism upon Christianity, a few have noted that "influence" was a two-way street, and that Christianity may have had at least as great an impact upon late paganism as the other way around.[3]

In any event, these observations are made largely by contemporary scholars. Occasionally, however, ancient commentators also noticed such parallels between Christianity and paganism. Celsus is a case in point. His observations, however, were not for the purpose of detecting "influence" in one direction or another. Rather, Celsus used these parallels as a weapon to attack his opponents, specifically to undermine Christian claims to exclusivism.

These "points of contact" appear frequently in Celsus' polemic as he compared Christianity with pagan religions in a number of areas. Eschatology provided important parallels; Celsus argued that the Christian doctrines of resurrection, heaven, and eternal punishment had counterparts in other religions. Jesus was like other pious men who had suffered nobly. The Christian refusal to worship images was similar to the iconoclasm observed in other cultures. In addition to providing parallels to accepted Greek and Roman beliefs, Celsus sometimes placed Christianity on the same level as other religious belief systems that he despised. His observation that the "barbaric" Scythians refused, like Christians, to worship images was not intended to compliment Christianity, but rather to provide the same kind of negative association that he used with regard to Judaism. For the most part, Celsus' comparisons served the purpose of exposing Christian teaching as unoriginal. If a doctrine or myth is similar to those belonging to other philosophies or religions, how can it claim to be the only valid one? Contrary to the claims of Christians about their uniqueness, Christianity was just another religion. Its claims to exclusivism were therefore unfounded and unreasonable.

Celsus' comparison of pagan and Christian ethics served the same purpose, as he refuted the common Christian apologetic argument that their ethical requirements and behavior were superior to those of the pagans. This argument was based upon the Christian adoption of the general features of the Jewish moral code as well as the teachings of Jesus, which had made ethical living a high priority for Christians; they were not slow to point out the differences they perceived between themselves and their pagan counterparts. From at least the middle of the first century CE, Christians characterized the "Gentiles" as being ruled by unrestrained sensuality:

> So I tell you this, and insist on it in the Lord, that you must no longer live as the Gentiles do, in the futility of their thinking. They are darkened in their understanding and separated from the life of God because of the ignorance that is in them due to the hardening of their hearts. Having lost all sensitivity, they have given themselves over to sensuality so as to indulge in every kind of impurity, with a continual lust for more. You, however, did not come to know Christ that way. . . .[4]

Later Christian writers argued against the immorality of pagan myth and philosophy. The Greek philosophers, they asserted, not the

Christians, were guilty of advocating cannibalism. The gods of pagan mythology routinely engaged in outrageous sexual behavior. How could pagans, whose sacred texts were full of such "abominations," accuse Christians of immorality? More than one apologist was willing to put Christian morality to the test, demanding that Christians be tried for actual crimes instead of merely claiming to be Christians. Justin had demanded of his pagan opponents "that the actions of all those denounced to you be judged, so that whoever is convicted may be punished as an offender, not as a Christian."[5]

Celsus criticized such an attitude on the part of the Christians by pointing out parallels with Greek philosophical ethics.

> Let us see also how [Celsus] thinks he can criticize our ethical teaching on the grounds that it is commonplace and in comparison with other philosophers contains no teaching that is impressive or new.[6]

Jesus' injunction to turn the other cheek, for example, was no different from the teaching of Socrates, while Christian "humility" was actually a corruption of Plato's ethics. Celsus' charge that Christian ethical teaching was "commonplace" was a direct rebuttal of his opponents' claim to possess a superior ethical system.

However, Celsus' rebuttal must be viewed not just from a theoretical viewpoint. The critic was not involved primarily in a debating game with Christians over ethical proof-texts from Plato and Jesus. Christian preachers were using their offer of a better way to live as an evangelizing strategy. As mentioned in the previous chapter, the fact that these evangelists were "invading" homes, convincing women and children to leave home and to come live with them, was highly disturbing to Celsus, especially as they were exhorting children

> . . .that they must not pay any attention to their father and school-teachers, but must obey them; they say that these talk nonsense and have no understanding, and that in reality they neither know nor are able to do anything good, but are taken up with mere empty chatter. But they alone, they say, know the right way to live, and if the children would believe them, they would become happy and make their home happy as well.[7]

According to Celsus, an important argument of Christian evangelists was their superior ethical teaching; they taught that pagan fathers and teachers were not only ignorant but incapable of doing good at all. Christianity promised a new and better way to live for those who would reject their inferior authority figures; happiness for the convert depended upon accepting a better way of life from the Christian teacher. Thus Celsus' argument against the uniqueness of Christian ethical teaching was intended in part to counter the claims of Christian evangelists. If Christian teaching could be exposed as nothing more than what was taught by the philosophers, or even as mere common decency, these claims could be undermined more effectively.

A final set of important parallels between Christian and pagan in the *True Doctrine* consists of Celsus' comparison of Jesus with other gods and heroes of Greek mythology. Such comparisons were not unique to Celsus. Part of the Christian apologetic strategy, since at least the time of Justin, was to argue that Christianity was, in some ways, not unusual at all. By comparing Jesus to familiar supernatural figures, Christians attempted to deflect criticism from the fact that they rejected other gods, and possibly to win acceptance. Justin in his *First Apology* argued the reasonableness of the crucifixion from the fact that many sons of Jupiter also suffered.

> . . .Aesculapius, who, though himself a healer of diseases, was struck by a thunderbolt and ascended into heaven; Bacchus, who was torn to pieces; Hercules, who rushed into the flames of the funeral pyre to escape his sufferings. . .[8]

Neither were Justin's comparisons limited to the death of Jesus and other divine figures. In the same way that Jesus was the Word of God, so also "Mercury is the angelic word of God"; like Perseus, Jesus was born of a virgin; like Asclepius, Jesus healed the lame, the paralytic, and the blind.

To be sure, the positive comparisons of Jesus to the gods make up only a minority of the references to the gods in Christian apologetic literature. For the most part the apologists of the second century and later criticized the immorality contained in the Greek and Roman myths, made sport of the Egyptian veneration of animals, and condemned the debauchery that occasionally characterized pagan worship. Christians adamantly rejected the gods, their myths, and the worship associated with them in no uncertain terms. Justin's tactic of positive comparison was simply an alternative way in which criticism could be deflected from the Christian worship of Jesus.

Although Celsus used the same type of comparisons, his motives, as we have stated, were quite different. A lengthy section[9] of *contra Celsum* has Origen and Celsus battling over the comparison of Jesus to other gods and heroes. Celsus listed and discussed numerous divine and human figures, such as Heracles, Dionysus and Asclepius, the last of whom was revered as a god since he both healed people and foretold the future. The purpose of this line of reasoning is clear: to demonstrate that Jesus was not unique among divine figures. Not only was Jesus similar to gods such as Asclepius, he was actually inferior; Asclepius' appearances after his death were clearer, longer-lasting, and witnessed by more people than those of the phantasmal Jesus. Celsus' argument attacked the uniqueness of Jesus by asserting that, even if he really did perform miracles and rise from the dead, he had plenty of other divine company. Although both Celsus and Justin compared Jesus to divine gods and heroes, Celsus' strategy served a different purpose from that of the apologist: to undermine Christian exclusivism by denying the uniqueness of his opponents' mythology.

That this was indeed Celsus' strategy is further evidenced by his comparison of Jesus with human figures such as Aristeas the Proconnesian, who vanished suddenly and reappeared; Abaris the Hyperborean, who carried an arrow throughout the world without stopping to eat; and Cleomedes the Astypalean, who locked himself inside a chest and disappeared when the chest was broken open.[10] Since these men did not come to be revered as gods even though they performed amazing feats, why should Jesus be worshiped after his alleged resurrection? Celsus trumped the argument of Christ's uniqueness by locating him as merely one among others. Thus Celsus attacked the uniqueness of Jesus on two fronts. In the first place, Jesus had divine company and was therefore not one of a kind, even if he really did perform miracles and rise from the dead. Second, Jesus had much more *human* company, those who were not considered worthy of worship, although they too performed fantastic deeds.

In this way Celsus argued that Christianity's claims to exclusivism, as reflected in the person of Jesus, were illegitimate. Since

Christ was not unique, he did not deserve to be treated as a unique being at the expense of other gods and heroes. It would be going too far to suggest that a non-exclusive Jesus would have nullified all of the criticism leveled at Christianity; the crucifixion alone provided an enormous amount of polemic fodder for Celsus and other opponents. We can, however, draw the conclusion that the uniqueness of the central figure of Christian mythology was an important target for Celsus' attack. Both pagans and Christians used arguments that denied the uniqueness of Jesus, albeit for different reasons. For Justin and other apologists, the comparison was meant to win respectability for the fledgling faith. In the case of Celsus, it had the aim of undermining the uniqueness, and thus the exclusiveness, of the religion he founded.

It may be asked whether, given Celsus' tendency to discredit every facet of Christianity, such a strategy was wise. Was Celsus falling into Justin's trap? In a way, the answer is "yes." Placing Jesus in company with the popular god of healing, for example, could have had the unintended effect of legitimizing the worship of the very man whose legitimacy he was attempting to deny. Celsus' development of such points of contact between Christian and pagan mythology may have served the polemic in the short term as an argument against Christian exclusivism, as was clearly his intent. However, this particular aspect of the *True Doctrine* illustrates one of the dangers inherent in attacking exclusivism: the risk of exposing more similarities between polemicist and opponent than was helpful for the larger strategy of the totalizing discourse.

Nor was this danger limited to the area of Christian mythology. Celsus' tactic of criticizing Christian exclusivism also targeted the larger issue of Christian revelation as found in the Bible. After all, could not the teachings of Christianity be found in the many belief systems already available? While we have already sampled this method of attack with regard to Christian ethical teaching, Celsus used it against the very concept of Christian revelation. Whatever claims they might have to the manifestation of divine truth, they were only partaking in what had already been revealed to the ancients long ago:

> [I]f a divine spirit came down from God to foretell the divine truths, this may be the spirit which declares these doctrines; indeed, it was because

men of ancient times were touched by this spirit that they proclaimed many excellent doctrines.[11]

Perhaps Celsus had no way of knowing that this statement would have been welcomed by many of his Christian opponents. That God had revealed truth to the rest of the world as well as to the Christians—primarily through Plato—made perfect sense to the majority of Christian writers from Justin in the second century to Eusebius in the fourth and beyond. They would continue to build intellectual bridges to pagan philosophy and religious belief, bridges which in the long term would contribute to the growing acceptance of Christianity.

The spirit of Neoplatonic thought in the third and fourth centuries would seek and welcome such bridges in its attempt to unify the disparate strands of philosophical and religious teaching in the empire. By demonstrating that there were important points of contact between Christianity and paganism, Celsus may unwittingly have contributed to Christianity's intellectual and religious acceptability. Although he himself did not blaze the trail leading to Christian assimilation into the conceptual environment of late antique paganism, he unknowingly stumbled upon the same path on his own way to a different destination.

Of the conceptual property that Christians shared with their pagan neighbors, the Platonist philosophical tradition was the most far-reaching in terms of the theological development of Christianity. However, long before the councils of the fourth and later centuries would take up Platonic philosophical categories in order to define particular aspects of the faith, Plato was being used in both the polemic and apologetic venues of pagan-Christian interaction. On the apologetic side, Justin had begun the project of Christian Platonism on a limited scale in the middle of the second century. By the early third century, Clement of Alexandria was engaged in a full-scale effort to reconcile the teachings of Christianity with Græco-Roman philosophy.

On the pagan side, philosophical considerations constitute an important element of Celsus' anti-Christian polemic. Their inclusion in the *True Doctrine* seems to have been designed to meet several goals. In the first place, it was necessary simply to refute publicly the claims of the Christians that their beliefs were worthy of acceptance. Further, Christian evangelists and apologists had insisted from the beginning that their faith was a plausible alternative to pagan religion; by 200 CE, however, they were presenting Christianity no longer as merely an alternative but as the logical culmination of Hellenistic philosophy and culture. Of course, the presentation of Christian teaching simultaneously as an alternative to the dominant world view and as its purest manifestation represents a profound contradiction, at least on the surface; it was a contradiction that Julian exploited relentlessly. However, it is the latter assertion, the attempted merging of Christian with pagan philosophical belief, that appears to have alarmed Celsus the most. To Celsus, the Christian blurring of the boundaries between their own doctrines and Græco-Roman thought was an intellectually intolerable exercise. He viewed his opponents' presentation of Platonism in Christian dress as a thinly disguised refutation of the most basic premises of common sense as well as philosophy. Thus a major element of Celsus' critique was an attempt to re-establish the boundaries between Christian "barbarism" and pagan thought.

The numerous attempts on the part of Celsus and his successors to establish and maintain these boundaries constituted such an important component of anti-Christian polemic that they are indispensable to any study of the literature. They formed a great deal of the intellectual battlefield during the third and fourth centuries; pagan critics would by and large attempt to marginalize Christianity by denying its aspiration to become a "philosophical sect." That Celsus was waging this battle near the beginning of the process and Julian after it was largely completed gives us valuable insight into the development of this important aspect of pagan-Christian relations. Here we address three areas of Christian belief that are philosophically important in the *True Doctrine:* the incarnation of Christ, the doctrine of the resurrection of the body, and Christian epistemology.

The incarnation of Christ was the element of Christian theology that Celsus attacked most fiercely; his argument against the doctrine was based upon what was assumed by virtually all the philosophical schools of the Greek world. The absolute transcendence of the ultimate deity had been central to Greek philosophy since Plato. Conversely, the inferiority of the material universe to the unseen divine world was a given; matter occupied the lowest level of both reality and goodness in the metaphysical hierarchy. Thus to Celsus, a Platonist, the idea of the incarnation represented an unthinkable move on the part of God from the realm of blessedness to that of corruption.

> Furthermore, [Celsus] says, let us take up the argument again with further proofs. I have nothing new to say, but only ancient doctrines. God is good and beautiful and happy, and exists in the most beautiful state. If then He comes down to men, He must undergo change, a change from good to bad, from beautiful to shameful, from happiness to misfortune, and from what is best to what is most wicked.[12]

While various aspects of philosophical theology had undergone changes over the previous centuries,[13] Celsus' summary of the "ancient doctrines" regarding the separation between God and the physical world of the senses was an important and commonly held theological assumption. The incarnation represented to Celsus a violation of the gulf between a transcendent deity and the inferior material world.

On the other hand, Christian apologists had argued that the incarnation was entirely reasonable since pagan myths were full of interaction between gods and the world. However, Christians did not claim to be associated ultimately with a deity on the level of Greek mythology; they claimed to be worshiping the supreme deity itself. Christians made no apologies for their belief that the object of their worship was the transcendent Platonic deity, even though, as discussed previously, they argued at the same time for the acceptance of their religion on the basis of the similarities between Jesus and the lower gods.

This theological double standard was not lost on Celsus or any of the other critics of Christianity. Christian apologists were not going to get away with disguising exclusivist monotheism as conventional mythology, even for the sake of argument. They could not have it both ways, trying on the one hand to win acceptability for Christianity by comparing Jesus to Asclepius while claiming on the other that their God was the supreme deity of Platonic philosophy. For Celsus, the incarnation provided the focal point of this contradiction and thus an important point of attack. The supreme deity of the Christians violated all the known rules of the universe by becoming matter; as far as Celsus was concerned, an incarnated supreme God was an oxymoron. The incarnation provided an important area in which Celsus attempted to draw a clear boundary between Christian teaching and Platonic thought.

The Christian belief in the resurrection of the body provided a second such area. Like the incarnation, the idea of a physical resurrection flew in the face of Platonic theology, which held that the material world occupied the lowest level of the divine hierarchy; physical resurrection, as opposed to the immortality of the soul, was not only repugnant but also theologically impossible. After calling Christian (and Jewish) hopes for a bodily resurrection "the hope of worms," Celsus went on to assert the contradiction that the idea of resurrection provided to any rational concept of deity.

> But, indeed, neither can God do what is shameful nor does He desire what is contrary to nature.... As for the flesh, which is full of things which it is not even nice to mention, God would neither desire nor be able to make it everlasting contrary to reason. For He Himself is the reason of everything that exists; therefore He is not able to do anything contrary to reason or to His own character.[14]

God's character included, naturally, the separation from matter. Any doctrine of a bodily resurrection, therefore, was anti-philosophical as well as impossible, Christian appeals to God's omnipotence notwithstanding. Besides the philosophical objection, the logical problem was equally popular with critics: what if a person died at sea, and his body then eaten by fish who were later eaten by birds? And what if the birds were later eaten by other people? How could such a person possibly undergo a physical resurrection? Arguments of this type augmented the philosophical objections to the Christian and Jewish belief in the resurrection.

As it happens, Origen, himself a Christian Platonist, had his own problems with the doctrine of the resurrection. For largely the same reasons as Celsus, he would resist the idea of a literal physical restoration of the body. Although the church eventually rejected this capitulation to Platonism, his stance on the issue reveals just how far some Christians were willing to go in order to present Christianity as philosophically plausible. Celsus, on the other hand, by presenting his opponents' view in its traditional form—the literal resurrection of the physical body—attempted to draw as sharp a distinction as possible between "common sense" Platonism and Christianity.

Celsus was also critical of Christian epistemology, the third major philosophical area to which he gave his attention. The specific ways by which God could be known varied through the development of Platonic philosophy, from Plato's own intellectual approach to the mystical union with the One advanced by Plotinus, the founder of Neoplatonism in the third century CE. One aspect that the different approaches to God had in common was their claim to be difficult, and thus their restriction to the philosophical elite. Whether God was to be comprehended by reason or by ascetic mysticism, the conception of God's separateness from the material world virtually mandated such a difficulty—the inadequacy of human knowledge and language to apprehend the divine.[15]

Although Celsus accused Christians of holding to a non-Platonic theology, it has been observed more recently that some early Christian teaching did indeed include Platonic descriptions of God, particularly in the Johannine literature.[16] References to God's invisibility are not infrequent in the Bible and were standard fare in early Christian theology. God's knowability, however, was quite another matter. Many of the Johannine statements affirming God's absolute transcendence are conditioned by affirmations that God can indeed be known, experienced, and loved, particularly through the intermediary agency of Jesus: "No one has ever seen God, but God the One and Only, who is at the Father's side, has made him known" (John 1:18). "No one has ever seen God; but if we love one another, God lives in us and his love is made complete in us" (1 John 4:12). Platonic, perhaps, in ontological transcendence, but not in accessibility.

Nonetheless, Celsus alleged that the Christian way of knowing God relied primarily upon the senses and not on the spirit.

Celsus again speaks as follows: "Again, too, they will say: 'How are they to know God unless they lay hold of him by sense-perception?'" He then gives an answer to this question, saying: "This utterance is not that of a man or of the soul, but of the flesh. Nevertheless let them listen to me, if so cowardly and carnal a race are able to understand anything. If you shut your eyes to the world of sense and look up with the mind, if you turn away from the flesh and raise the eyes of the soul, only so will you see God.[17]

Celsus' epistemological dualism attempted to strike a blow at the Christian knowledge of God by attributing such "knowledge" to the flesh rather than to the superior faculties of the mind and spirit. After all, the Christian faith depended ultimately upon the reports given by the apostles who claimed to have seen him. Had Celsus been familiar with the Johannine epistles, 1 John 1:1 would have provided especially useful material against which to argue.

That which was from the beginning, which we have heard, which we have seen with our eyes, which we have looked at and our hands have touched— this we proclaim concerning the Word of Life.

In any event, according to Celsus, Jesus' perception of God at his baptism and the reports of Jesus' post-resurrection appearances were equally invalid, since they were most likely the product of hallucination or magical apparition.[18]

Christian epistemology was thus inferior to the Platonic ideal of "raising the eyes of the soul" in order to see God. Later, quoting Plato's *Timaeus*, Celsus argued that knowing God is extremely difficult, even for the wisest of philosophers: "Now to find the Maker and father of this universe is difficult, and after finding him it is impossible to declare him to all men." Surely, if the knowledge of God was difficult for the wisest of people, it would be impossible for the "carnal race" of Christians. Celsus concluded that not only was it impossible for Christians to comprehend God, it would be difficult for them even to follow his argument on the matter.

Such "ignorance" on the part of his opponents is a common theme in the *True Doctrine*. Celsus frequently translated the theme into the charge that Christians were uneducated and of low social class. According to the polemicist, Christians were only able to convince slaves, women and children of their doctrines; they consciously shunned the wise and sought only foolish and ignorant people to add to their numbers. It seems clear that Celsus was familiar with at least a paraphrase of Paul's rhetoric in the first chapter of 1 Corinthians 1:

Where is the wise man? Where is the scholar? Where is the philosopher of this age? Has not God made foolish the wisdom of the world? For since in the wisdom of God the world through its wisdom did not know him, God was pleased through the foolishness of what was preached to save those who believe.... For the foolishness of God is wiser than man's wisdom, and the weakness of God is stronger than man's strength.[19]

Christians claimed that the knowledge of God was not only simple, but, according to Paul, actually in opposition to philosophical wisdom.

Celsus took this line of Pauline rhetoric—which was originally an argument for the superiority of God's wisdom to that of the world—and transformed it into a polemic weapon against the "ignorance and foolishness" of the Christians. Celsus' line of argument, however, was not merely intended to score polemic points against Christians by relegating them to the lower social classes. Embedded in the fabric of his overall criticism of Christian ignorance is an important epistemological argument. Since it is difficult for even the wise to know God, he argued, how much more difficult—indeed, impossible—must it be for Christians? Celsus found ridiculous the Christian claim that only faith, not rational argument, was required for the knowledge of God. This approach violated Platonic sensibilities regarding apprehension of the One. Such Christian anti-intellectualism, combined with the alleged ignorance and social status of Christians, was enough to dismiss out of hand their claim to be a cult of the highest God. According to Celsus, it was ludicrous to claim that barbarians (such as the Jews), the lower class (such as the Christians), and the fideistic approach of Christian evangelists could apprehend what only the wisest philosophers could even begin to grasp.

Such an epistemological inversion on the part of the Christians was not only counterintuitive but philosophically offensive to Celsus. His characterization of Christians as occupying the lowest strata of society served more than merely a polemic function. The social issue was important not only for the sake of rhetoric, but also because Platonic epistemology allowed the knowledge of God only for the wisest. His argument thus served both rhetorical and theological functions, based as it was in Platonic "elite" epistemology. Celsus was attempting to marginalize Christianity, both socially and philosophically, a task of no small importance since Christianity was making inroads among the upper classes at the time he wrote the *True Doctrine.*

Celsus' distinctions between Christian doctrine and Greek philosophy would have been intended primarily for the elite among his readers. He himself said as much, particularly when polemicizing against those whom he characterized as his lesser-educated opponents. Of course, his arguments were not meant to be read only by philosophers; the time-honored question as to the reconstitution of scattered human remains at the resurrection was popular anti-Christian fare. For the most part, however, the philosophical criticisms we have examined thus far would have been most intelligible to the more educated.

Celsus' defense of polytheism, however, would have been understandable both to the elite and to the general public. Everyone from agricultural laborer to court philosopher was involved in the worship of the gods to one degree or another. The festivals of the gods were important social occasions. Every Roman home honored its *genius,* as well as its *lares* and *penates* as guardians of home and pantry respectively. The philosophical elite, while privately (and occasionally publicly) criticizing the more outrageous elements of Greek and Roman mythology, would not have dreamed of neglecting civic cult. Thus Celsus' attack on Christian exclusive monotheism would have been relevant for a broad audience.

But the gods of antiquity were not merely beings to be worshiped with the appropriate public and private ceremonies. The gods permeated the universe, infusing the physical world with life and mediating between the realms of matter and spirit. To Plutarch in the second century CE, ignoring these "daemons" could lead only to chaos, just as if the air were removed from the space between the earth and the moon.

> . . .just in the same way those who refuse to leave us the race of demigods [δαιμόνων] make the relations of gods and men remote and alien by doing away with the "interpretive and ministering nature" as Plato has called it, or else they force us to a disorderly confusion of all things, in which we bring the god into men's emotions and activities, drawing him down to our needs. . . .[20]

The "ministering spirits" provided not only cosmological order but also the necessities of human life. Ignoring these lower gods was a supreme act of ingratitude, according to Celsus, with potentially disastrous results if they were not kept satisfied.

> But whenever [Christians] eat food, and drink wine, and taste fruits, and drink even water itself, and breathe even the very air, are they not receiving each of these from certain daemons, among whom the administration of each of these has been divided? . . . Either we ought not to live at all anywhere on earth and not to enter this life, or, if we do enter this life under these conditions, we ought to give thanks to the daemons who have been allotted control over earthly things, and render to them firstfruits and prayers as long as we live that we may obtain their goodwill towards us.[21]

At the same time, however, it was not sufficient for Celsus simply to affirm the validity of traditional polytheism; he employed other theological tools already in circulation. There existed, for example, a pagan "monotheism," confined for the most part to philosophical circles. At least since Plato, it had become necessary to work out the relationship between the supreme being of philosophical construct and the many gods of the Græco-Roman pantheon; the same problem would arise for the gods of the various nations that would eventually be subsumed under the Roman Empire.[22] Celsus' challenge was to critique Christian monotheistic exclusivism while simultaneously preserving the basic concept of philosophical "monotheism." His solution was that the various gods were responsible for the differing operations of the universe at the behest of the One.

> And whatever there may be in the universe, whether the work of God, or of angels, or of other daemons or heroes, do not all these things keep a law given by the greatest God? And has there not been appointed over each particular thing a being who has been thought worthy to be allotted power? Would not a man, therefore, who worships God rightly worship the being who has obtained authority from him?[23]

For Celsus, the worship of the gods was necessary not only in order to keep the blessings of the physical universe flowing to humanity;

the proper veneration of those deities was the correct way to worship the supreme God as well. More specific benefits were available to devotees of particular gods; healing, children, or protection from danger might be bestowed by deities who received adequate veneration from a worshiper.[24] The gods served as agents of the supreme God, operating the mechanisms of the physical world and preserving harmony in nature. They were worthy of worship according to the traditions handed down from one's ancestors.

But Celsus did not stop with affirming a theoretical relationship of the many to the One. The supreme deity could be accessed (imperfectly, of course) through some of the avenues afforded by popular religion; in this he was in agreement with other writers of his era. With the emergence of a large empire had come an impetus to unify the disparate strands of particular national religions, on a popular as well as philosophical level. One such attempt in the realm of popular religion was made in the second century by Lucius Apuleius in his story *The Golden Ass*. In this tale the protagonist, who has been turned into a donkey, receives a vision of the Egyptian goddess Isis on the beach near the Greek port city of Cenchreae. In the vision, the goddess assumes sweeping power and authority.

> I am she that is the natural mother of all things, mistress and governess of all the elements, the initial progeny of worlds, chief of the powers divine, queen of all that are in hell, the principal of them that dwell in heaven, manifested alone and under one form of all the gods and goddesses. At my will the planets of the sky, the wholesome winds of the seas, and the lamentable silences of hell be disposed; my name, my divinity is adored throughout all the world, in divers manners, in variable customs, and by many names.[25]

Isis makes two remarkable claims for herself here. The first is universal supremacy over all the powers of the universe. While not explicitly stating her supreme status in terms of Platonic monotheism, the goddess claims a broad range of powers and a high status of rulership that more than hints at universal supremacy. The second notable trait is that she claims to be worshiped "in divers manners, in variable customs, and by many names." Isis asserts that at least some of the gods and goddesses of the different nations are in reality to be identified with a particular deity, namely herself.

Apuleius is, of course, doing more than writing a fanciful tale about a man turned into a donkey and then restored by the power of Isis. The story is an undisguised attempt to advocate the cult of Isis by demonstrating her power, mercy and universality. It also appears to have been an attempt to reconcile on a popular level the notion of a transcendent deity with the varieties of pagan religion practiced by the people. It has been argued that Apuleius was heavily indebted to Plutarch, particularly his work *On Isis and Osiris*, which attempted to reconcile Platonist monotheism with popular religion by asserting the ultimate compatibility of Isis worship with Platonism.[26]

Even if Celsus himself was not a devotee of Isis, he would have been sympathetic to the claims of Apuleius' "universally pluralistic" goddess. Although she claimed to be the supreme deity, she did not deny the existence or the value of the other gods. She even welcomed the adoration she received through these gods throughout the world, even though such adoration was not directed specifically to her. All belief systems were valid because they ultimately pointed to her, whether or not this fact was universally realized. In the same way, Celsus was not alone in holding that differing belief systems could be valid; the greatest authority, after all, was the witness of antiquity. One of Celsus' contemporaries, Numenius of Apamea, had a respect for ancient national religions, a respect that led him to contemplate the unity the religions of the world might have in common. According to Numenius, all religions contained truth since they came ultimately from the same source.

> But when one has spoken upon this point, and sealed it by the testimonies of Plato, it will be necessary to go back and connect it with the precepts of Pythagoras, and to appeal to the nations of good repute, bringing forward their rites and doctrines, and their institutions which are formed in agreement with those of Plato, all that the Brachmans, and Jews, and Magi, and Egyptians arranged.[27]

For Celsus, there was nothing inherently wrong with monotheism—an inclusive monotheism, at any rate—since many nations, particularly the oldest and wisest, possessed the concept as it was embedded in their national myths. In agreement with Apuleius and

Numenius, Celsus asserted that the supreme deity could be called by any of the names ascribed to him by the various nations, since the existence of such a God had been universally perceived from antiquity. Thus Zeus could be called Zen, Adonai, Sabaoth, the Egyptian Amoun, or even the Scythian Papaeus. This assertion, however, was more than a statement about what the divinity ought to be named. It was a theological statement that informed what Celsus called the "true doctrine," the fact that "There is an ancient doctrine which has existed from the beginning, which has always been maintained by the wisest nations and cities and wise men."[28] While the content of the "true doctrine" cannot be completely reconstructed from Origen's recapitulation of Celsus' teaching,[29] what seems to have been important to Celsus was that such a teaching dated from earliest antiquity and was common to many nations (not including, of course, the Jews, *contra* Numenius).

Naturally, for Celsus, the existence of such a "true doctrine" in no way detracted from the necessity of worshiping the traditional gods. Even a devotee of Isis would have participated in domestic cult and the festivals of the civic deities. The bottom line for Celsus was that the lesser gods ought not to be neglected, regardless of what "ultimate" truth might actually be with regard to the identity of a supreme God.

Complementing Celsus' belief in a "universal polytheism" was his doctrine that the supreme God had assigned "overseers" to the nations, deities that came to be identified with the various geographic regions and ethnic groups and that were responsible for their welfare. Such a theology accomplished several purposes. In the first place, it explained the variations in religious practice among the nations, since each nation's gods had differing requirements for worship. At the same time, this construction perpetuated the ethical imperative that everyone ought to follow the traditions of their ancestors, since the various nations and peoples were still under the oversight of the gods that were originally appointed over them.

> . . .it is probable that from the beginning the different parts of the earth were allotted to different overseers, and are governed in this way by having been divided between certain authorities. In fact, the practices done by each nation are right when they are done in the way that pleases the overseers; and it is impious to abandon the customs which have existed in

each locality from the beginning.[30]

The polemic context of Celsus' theology was, of course, his assertion that everyone should worship the gods, particularly those of
one's own nation. That the Christians were guilty of apostasy—not
only from Judaism but from the ancestral religions of their respective Gentile nations—is a prominent theme in the *True Doctrine;* the
teaching regarding the national divine overseers gave Celsus the
theological justification he needed for calling the Christians back to
their religious roots. At the same time, it also offered the critic a
way to meet his objective discussed earlier, namely to attack the exclusive Christian version of monotheism while preserving at the
same time a Platonic universalism.

By presenting Christianity as incompatible with either popular
polytheism or Platonic monotheism—or, in this case, a combination
of both—Celsus attempted rhetorically to marginalize Christianity
out of existence. According to Celsus, although Plato and the gods
could coexist peacefully, it was impossible to integrate Christian
teaching into any valid theological system, whether philosophical
or popular. That a Greek writer in the Severan age of the Roman
empire found himself defending basic polytheism is not inconsequential, perhaps an indicator of the underlying strength of Christian
exclusive monotheism.

Celsus wrote the *True Doctrine* at a time during which Christianity was undergoing profound changes. It was transforming itself
from a state of relative isolation to a level of social and intellectual
integration with pagan culture. A high conversion rate was break-
ing down the barriers between church and society. The church was
continuing to define itself in relation to Judaism, a process accelerated by two Jewish revolts and the Marcionite movement. Clement
of Alexandria was beginning the process of marrying Christian theology with Greek philosophy. And even though persecution
continued in varying degrees for the next hundred years, the third
century witnessed the growth of Christianity into a major religious
force.

Such was the Christianity with which Celsus grappled. It was a
complex and growing, not to mention divided, organism. For this
reason it is important to look critically at Celsus' representation of

his opponents in order to describe his rhetorical strategy. Some aspects of the polemic of the *True Doctrine* appear somewhat strained. These include Celsus' characterization of Christianity as a secretive, isolated offshoot of Judaism, as well as his caricature of Christians as ignorant, foolish and unphilosophical. Scholars have normally characterized Celsus as a learned critic of Christianity, and there is little doubt that he researched his opponent with some care. Although his actual knowledge of the Bible seems to have been limited, especially compared with that of Porphyry and Julian, his criticism of Christianity was in large measure based on observation and careful reflection. However, scholarship on Celsus has historically tended to treat him as an impartial observer, perhaps forgetting that his was a polemic work intended for rhetorical effect, not a record for church historians of a later era. For this reason he is sometimes read uncritically as his excerpts in Origen's *contra Celsum* are mined for historical information regarding the early church.

A better model for interpreting Celsus' attack on Christianity takes into account his polemic context. The church near the turn of the third century was emerging from its isolation with vigor; rumors of immoral behavior were no longer sufficient to oppose it. A new strategy was therefore necessary, one that Celsus applied so successfully that such a mind as Origen's was needed to refute it a half century later. Christianity presented such an overwhelming threat to Celsus and the world he valued that a written work was required to refute the church's claims, ridicule its beliefs, and marginalize its adherents. For this reason, Celsus adopted a rhetorical stance designed to erect an impenetrable rhetorical boundary between Christianity and paganism, between the church and society, a fenced enclosure within which he could isolate and display his opponents in an exaggerated fashion. His totalizing discourse allowed no positive characterizations of Christianity; even the similarities between Jesus and Asclepius and the other gods were intended to accentuate the irrationality of Christian exclusivism. Celsus was inaccurate, but with good reason. His presentation of Christianity as "huddled in a corner" was a reaction to the fact that Christians had begun to emerge from that corner in force.

At the same time, although Celsus' critique lacked the accusations of sexual immorality and cannibalism that characterized the previous decades, it retained something important in common with the shouts of the crowds at the amphitheaters of Lyons and Vienne. The *True Doctrine* contains no hint that Christianity was tolerable in any form, whether social, mythical or doctrinal; Celsus' goal, like that of the crowd, was the elimination of Christianity altogether. In this respect, although his criticism was more philosophical in tone and content than previous critiques had been, he nonetheless carried the banner for the early phase in the pagan criticism of Christianity, a phase characterized by a totalizing discourse of unconditional rejection.

In spite of Christianity's moves toward cultural integration, Celsus denied his opponents, or any aspect of their belief system, any measure of intellectual or theological legitimacy. Regardless of the prevailing philosophical and religious impetus (as well as his own tendency) to unite all religious belief into a "unified" theology, Celsus resisted the trend when it came to the Jews and Christians. Although he was not ready to surrender any ground of legitimacy to either his opponents or their Jewish spiritual ancestors, the currents of universalism were already gaining strength by the time Celsus put down his pen. The rhetorical boundary that both he and Tertullian were attempting to construct between Christianity and pagan theology was already being eroded by 200 CE; Clement of Alexandria in particular was identifying in very specific terms the similarities between the Christian faith and the "truth-loving Plato." The boundary would disintegrate further over the next hundred years; by the time of Constantine it would be barely recognizable.

4

Porphyry and the Polemic of Universalism

Celsus' criticisms went unanswered until about 248 CE, when Origen composed *contra Celsum* at the request of his friend Ambrose. By that time, however, the relationship between Christians and the dominant pagan culture had undergone enormous changes. Gone for good were the lingering rumors of cannibalism and ritual sex. If a wave of conversions had indeed occurred in the late second and early third centuries, their children and grandchildren were now swelling the ranks of the church. A few of these, Origen himself among them, were enjoying access to the imperial court. According to the philosopher Porphyry, whose criticism of Christianity is the subject of this chapter, Origen was also at one time a colleague of Plotinus, the founder of Neoplatonism. To be sure, only the Christian elite possessed such philosophical sophistication; the greater part of the church still consisted of the uneducated, and Celsus' criticism of the Christian underclass maintained some degree of validity through the third century. However, Christians had not only begun the process of appropriating Greek philosophy for themselves, they were also making converts among the upper classes. Over the course of the third century the church was becoming a more respectable, as well as permanent, fixture in Roman society.

From the perspective of many pagans, such respectability demanded new forms of opposition; in their view Christianity had become a serious problem to the empire. Popular resentment was expressed in 249 with anti-Christian riots in Alexandria, the first in many decades. An edict of the emperor Decius in 250 requiring everyone in the empire to sacrifice to the gods precipitated the first persecution of Christianity that was both imperially directed and widely enforced. Large numbers of Christians sacrificed, and many were killed before Decius died in battle against the Goths in 251.

In about 270, new literary opposition to Christianity appeared from the Neoplatonic philosopher Porphyry of Tyre (c. 233–c. 305). His knowledge of Christianity, especially his familiarity with the Bible, was much greater than that of Celsus. At the same time, the target of his polemic had become a more formidable presence than Celsus' opponents had been. As a result, some of Porphyry's arguments demonstrate an acceptance of, or at least resignation to, the permanent presence of Christianity, with an accompanying shift in rhetorical strategy. Before we proceed, however, a more detailed look at the context of the third century is in order.

During the late second and early third centuries the empire enjoyed relative peace under the Severan dynasty (193–235). Massive building projects were completed during this period. The imperial court was a place of intellectual and religious exchange, a phenomenon associated particularly with Julia Domna, the wife of emperor Septimius Severus and daughter of the Syrian high priest of the Baal of Emesa.

Christians continued to suffer sporadic persecution through the first decade of the third century; despite, or perhaps because of, the growth of the church during this period, many regarded Christianity as a threat of increasing seriousness. However, there are a number of differences between the persecutions of this period and those of a generation earlier. The accusations of outrageous immorality, namely the charges of cannibalism and ritual intercourse, are not found in the surviving literature. Instead, the accounts of the martyrdoms contain more prominently the charges that the Christians had abandoned the gods and that they refused to perform sacrifice to them on behalf of the emperor.

One aspect of the persecutions of the early third century, however, testifies to the fact that the Christian presence had been accepted as a permanent fact of life. In many of the martyrologies the victims were new converts, while most church leaders seem to have been left alone. In Alexandria, for example, several students of Origen were executed during the reign of Septimius Severus, while Origen himself lived until 254, when he died from the torture he had undergone during the later persecution of Decius. The reason converts were singled out may have been the decree that Septimius Severus is reported to have issued forbidding conversion to either Judaism or Christianity. Such a decree (if genuine) reveals that although conversion was prohibited, the actual existence of Christianity had become an accepted reality by the early years of the third century. The two decades that followed the Severan persecution were relatively peaceful for the church; in fact, much of the written evidence suggests that the imperial courts were actually becoming sympathetic to Christians. Whether or not is it true, as the writer of the *Augustan History* reports, that the emperor Alexander Severus (222–235) kept statues of Orpheus, Abraham and Christ in his private chapel,[1] the fact that such a rumor could be sustained attests to a greater acceptability for Christianity than would have been dreamed of under Marcus Aurelius. In any event, the emperor's mother Julia Mamaea held discussions with Origen at Alexandria, another indication that Christian beliefs were at least receiving a hearing at the highest levels.

The death of Alexander Severus in 235 marked the beginning of a nearly total dissolution of the Roman Empire. Incursions from barbarians threatened normally safe urban areas, including Athens. Invasions by the newly-revived Persian Empire under Sapor I brought chaos to the eastern parts of the empire. A series of plagues, famines, natural disasters and short-lived soldier-emperors made life more precarious than at any time in the history of the empire; the fifth-century pagan historian Zosimus was not exaggerating when he declared that "the entire Roman Empire [was] reeling in the direction of ultimate annihilation."[2]

In this threatening environment scapegoats were sought and found in the Christians. In such an atmosphere of crisis, the perception that the gods had abandoned the empire fed public animosity toward the Christians. Even the reign of an emperor sympathetic to Christianity, Philip the Arab (244–249), only delayed the inevitable outbreak of official action.

Such action was taken by Decius, emperor from 249 to 251. In an unprecedented move for unprecedented times, he ordered everyone in the empire to sacrifice to the gods of Rome. Nor were Christian leaders spared as they had been under Severus. Fabian, bishop of Rome, fell to the decree, as did Alexander at Jerusalem and Babylas at Antioch. Dionysius, bishop of Alexandria, was captured by authorities but was later rescued by Christians; in Carthage, Cyprian went into hiding. This time, the motives for the persecution were unmistakable; the disasters of the third century were

blamed, if not on the Christians, then upon the failure of the population to adhere to the traditional gods. That the Christians were a
major cause of this neglect was lost on no one.

Large numbers of Christians sacrificed to the gods of Rome; several decades of relative peace had brought many into the church
who were unprepared for martyrdom. If Dionysius' account of
events at Alexandria is representative of the situation throughout
the empire, the persecution produced many apostates as well as
martyrs.

> All, indeed, were greatly alarmed, and many of the more eminent imme-
> diately gave way to [the edicts requiring sacrifice]. . . others were brought
> by their acquaintance, and when called by name, they approached the
> impure and unholy sacrifices. But, pale and trembling, as if they were not
> to sacrifice, but themselves to be the victims of the sacrifices to the idols,
> they were jeered by many of the surrounding multitude, and were obvi-
> ously equally afraid to die and to offer the sacrifice. But some advanced
> with greater readiness to the altars, and boldly asserted that they had never
> before been Christians.[3]

The church's success in gaining converts had outrun the success of
discipline. Large amounts of church property were also confiscated,
a sign that the wealth of the church had increased dramatically since
the beginning of the century. Thus the Decian persecution is in some
ways an indicator of the success that Christianity had enjoyed in the
decades since the early Severan age.

The persecution was short-lived, however, as the emperor himself was killed in battle in 251. A few years later, in 257, the emperor
Valerian launched sporadic persecutions; Decius' edict had not
changed the basic perception linking the Christians with the disasters befalling the empire. The Christians had neglected the gods,
and therefore the gods had neglected the empire. One magistrate,
Aemilianus the deputy prefect of Egypt, went to the heart of the
matter during the interrogation of bishop Dionysius: "But who pre-
vents you from worshipping this one God, if he is a god, together
with those that are the natural gods?"[4] Christian exclusivism, expressed in their refusal to give proper honor to the gods, brought
Christians into direct conflict with the state.

The collapse of the empire was arrested during the reign of

Aurelian (270–275). His rule witnessed what may be rightly called the restoration of the empire, with the emperor himself known as the "restorer of the world." The Goths were beaten back from their incursions into the Italian peninsula and Greece, the earlier boundaries of the empire largely restored. Only Dacia was given up permanently, while an independent state that had arisen in Gaul was reabsorbed into the empire. In the east, Aurelian brought down Queen Zenobia of Palmyra in Syria, who had declared independence and had also conquered Egypt. Aurelian's reign was cut short when soldiers assassinated him in 275.

Decius and Valerian had failed to destroy Christianity, and the religion continued to gain converts and prestige during the dark years of the middle of the third century. The church's success in gaining converts and acquiring property has already been mentioned. Further evidence that Christianity had won a degree of acceptance was the affair of Paul of Samosata, bishop of Antioch (261–272). Called by other eastern bishops to account for his belief that the Logos had descended upon the person of Jesus rather than Jesus having been the Logos from conception, Paul was eventually condemned by a church council in 268. His removal from office was delayed, however, as long as Queen Zenobia held the city. When Aurelian captured Antioch in 272, the bishops took their case to the emperor, who decreed that the bishopric would be retained by "whom the Christian bishops of Italy and Rome should write."[5] Paul's subsequent removal was thus indirectly a result of an imperial decision.

While Aurelian's intervention in the controversy over the bishops is sometimes attested as a forerunner to Byzantine imperial involvement in doctrinal issues, it is better not to imply such a precedent from this event. For Aurelian, what was at issue was the restoration of church property to its rightful owners, not the settlement of a doctrinal dispute. More important to observe from this affair is that Christianity had been accepted by now as a permanent presence. The fact that a decision of bishops was accepted by an emperor who was not a Christian sympathizer is an even greater indication of pagan (or at least imperial) resignation to the presence of the church. The existence of Christianity, once precarious, was now permanent.

A final development should be summarized before proceeding

to Porphyry's polemic. In addition to reunifying the empire and restoring its territorial integrity, Aurelian undertook sweeping religious reforms. Important for the purposes of this study is what these reforms indicate about developments in the religious environment over the course of the third century, the substance of which developments are also reflected in Porphyry's writings.

Early in his reign Aurelian instituted a cult of the Sun in Rome[6] as an attempt to unify the religion of the empire after a lengthy period of chaos. Part of this unification involved a strengthening of the imperial cult as well; he was the first Roman emperor to proclaim his own divinity on official documents. His institution of the solar cult, however, represented the first major attempt to assimilate the disparate gods of the various parts of the empire under the authority of a single deity, *Sol Invictus* (The Unconquered Sun). While Franz Cumont's claim[7] that Aurelian's reforms constituted the death blow to traditional paganism is exaggerated, the rise of the solar cult was a key development in the general trend toward syncretism during the third century.

This syncretism on the imperial level occurred simultaneously with the career of the Neoplatonic philosopher Porphyry of Tyre, who articulated similar beliefs and who wrote *Against the Christians* in the same year as Aurelian's accession to the throne. What the emperor would attempt officially was already *au courant* in intellectual circles, at least on the abstract level. As we will observe, Porphyry's anti-Christian work gives us tantalizing if incomplete clues to a religious world view that could have, at least theoretically, even included elements of Christianity.

In 270 CE Porphyry wrote an extensive polemic against Christianity in fifteen books. What little remains is preserved exclusively in the works of later Christian authors. Many of Porphyry's criticisms of the Christians and their faith were anticipated by Celsus decades before. Like Celsus, Porphyry ridiculed the Christian beliefs in the incarnation, crucifixion, and resurrection of Jesus, for largely the same reasons as his predecessor. To Porphyry as to Celsus, the doctrine of hell was equally offensive; quoting the saying of Jesus, "With what measure you mete, it shall be measured to you again," Porphyry protested that the Christian teaching regarding eternal punishment for relatively limited sins did not fit Jesus' own fair criterion for judgment.

One area in which Porphyry exceeded Celsus, however, was in his knowledge of the Christian scriptures. Celsus appears to have had little familiarity with either the Jewish or Christian sacred writings; while he seemed familiar enough with many Christian beliefs and practices, he used very little of the Bible in his *True Doctrine*. Porphyry, on the other hand, was intimately familiar with the Bible of the Christians. In fact, of the 97 fragments that Adolf von Harnack assigned to the text of *Against the Christians*, about three-fourths deal directly or indirectly with the biblical text. It is perhaps this familiarity that led the fifth-century church historian Socrates to believe that Porphyry had at one time been a Christian. Porphyry's expertise in textual matters is also indicated by his evaluation of some of the gnostic writings:

> Many of the Christians of this period. . . exhibited also Revelations bearing the names of Zoroaster, Zostrianus, Nicotheus, Allogenes, Mesus, and others of that order. . . . I myself have shown on many counts that the Zoroastrian volume is spurious and modern, concocted by the sectaries in order to pretend that the doctrines they had embraced were those of the ancient sage.[8]

As for the texts of non-gnostic Christians, Porphyry argued that the biblical book of Daniel was "spurious and modern" as well. In an attempt to undermine Christian claims concerning the value of their predictive prophecies, he assigned the writing of Daniel to the reign of Antiochus Epiphanes, four centuries later than the traditional date of the sixth century BCE.[9]

While Porphyry's attacks on Daniel have received the most scholarly attention, the majority of his surviving criticisms of the Bible deal with the New Testament. His primary aim was to undermine the credibility of the New Testament by attacking the writers of the four gospels, the apostle Paul and his writings, and the apostles as a group. In addition, his attack on the apostles parallels in some respects Celsus' attack on Jesus. According to Porphyry the disciples of Jesus were deceitful magicians who tricked their hearers, especially women and the poor, for personal gain. "Rustic men and paupers, because they had nothing, worked certain wonders with magic arts. There is nothing to boast about in performing won-

ders."[10] Like the Jesus of Celsus' *True Doctrine,* the disciples were
cowardly and weak. With regard to their preaching and their reports of Jesus' life they were nothing more than sophists, plagiarists
and storytellers. It is for this reason that the Christian scriptures,
according to Porphyry, were unreliable and contradictory.

However, Porphyry had concerns other than attacking Christianity for its own sake. Unlike many philosophers, Porphyry was a
religious man, devoted to popular cult as well as philosophy. Historically, the philosophical tradition had in many ways been
unsympathetic to the religious beliefs and practices of most people.
In Porphyry, however, we find a unique fusion of religious and philosophical passions. His work *Philosophy from Oracles* was designed,
as the title indicates, to demonstrate the compatibility between the
Greek philosophical tradition and the approved oracles of the Mediterranean world.

With regard to his work *Against the Christians,* Timothy Barnes
has suggested[11] that Porphyry wrote it in the era of 300–305 CE as a
propagandistic effort to support the Great Persecution of 303–311,
although our study accepts the more commonly held date of 270.[12]
While it is possible that the uncovering of contradictions in the Christian scriptures—the primary constituents of the extant portions of
Porphyry's work—might serve political interests, what remains of
Against the Christians appears to be more a criticism of texts than
substantive attacks on a religion threatening to overwhelm the empire. To whatever degree the two issues can be legitimately
separated, Porphyry's concerns were more religious than political.

They were also more religious than philosophical in orientation.
Whereas it is true, as noted earlier, that Porphyry showed concerns
similar to those of Celsus, what survives of Porphyry's work is not
nearly so philosophically oriented as that of his predecessor. In fact,
Porphyry's assault on Christianity appears philosophically weak in
comparison to Celsus' *True Doctrine.* Even though he criticized such
doctrines as the resurrection of the dead, the majority of what survives of *Against the Christians* treats difficulties and contradictions
in the Christian scriptures, not arguments that the religion was philosophically objectionable.

Porphyry's relative lack of an explicitly Platonist point of depar-
ture is only one of a number of differences between his work and
that of Celsus. A further examination of these differences will assist

us in tracing not only the development of anti-Christian arguments in general over the course of the third century, but also the development of the opposition to Christian exclusivism. We have mentioned briefly a few of these differences, such as Porphyry's greater knowledge of the New Testament. Some of the major remaining differences reflect the progress of the church in society during the intervening period; others are a result of a better-informed opponent in the person of Porphyry of Tyre.

Perhaps the most apparent difference between the works of the two critics is Porphyry's complete lack of reference to Christian social exclusivism. This lack is a result of the increased diffusion of Christians into the larger society; by the middle of the third century Christians occupied positions in the army and in the upper echelons of society, including the imperial court. Gone for good were the days of the "secret society" that Celsus had criticized. Christians were meeting in the open, driven underground only during times of persecution; the construction of church buildings in the third century attests both the growing wealth and increasing public presence of Christians. The discovery at Dura Europos of the earliest known church building, dating from about 232 CE, indicates that Christianity enjoyed a measure of tolerance and wealth during the reign of Alexander Severus.

Lacking also in Porphyry's polemic is the criticism of Judaism so prevalent in Celsus' work. Celsus' treatment of Judaism and the Jewish scriptures had served the purpose of linking the Christians in an unfavorable manner with the "irrational" and "antisocial" religion that gave them birth; by attacking Judaism he thus attacked Christianity. Porphyry's discussions of the Hebrew Bible, on the other hand, did not generally criticize Judaism *per se*. Instead, his treatment of the Jewish scriptures was designed primarily to refute specifically Christian interpretations. While it is true that Porphyry sometimes attacked the Hebrew Bible, more typical of his polemic was his criticism of Christian allegorical interpretations of it, particularly on the part of Origen. Porphyry commented that Christian interpreters,

> ambitious rather to find some solution to the absurdities of the Jewish writings, instead of abandoning them, have turned their minds to expositions, inconsistent with themselves, and inapplicable to the writings. . .[13]

Porphyry was more concerned with Christian "mishandling" of the Hebrew Bible than with discrediting the Jewish writings themselves.

As alluded to earlier, another important development in *Against the Christians* is that Porphyry had a far better command of the New Testament than did Celsus. Although scholars often characterize Celsus as an informed opponent of Christianity, his knowledge of the Gospels was at times erroneous, seemingly based more on rumor than upon actual study. His understanding of the epistles was vague at best. There are few references to Pauline material, for instance, in the *True Doctrine,* and there is no mention of Paul in his work.[14] His literary successor Porphyry, however, seems to have read the Gospels and even the rest of the New Testament with some care. His detailed refutation of contradictions between Gospel accounts, for example, as well as his arguments against specific teachings of Jesus and Paul reveal an opponent of Christianity much more familiar with Christian writings than was Celsus.

Finally, perhaps the most intriguing element of Porphyry's work is the philosopher's assertion that, according to a prophetic oracle, the gods had elevated Jesus to the status of one of the immortals. While this development will be discussed in more detail later, it will suffice for the moment to observe that while Celsus' treatment of Jesus was exclusively negative, Porphyry attributed both immortality and piety to the founder of Christianity. And while it is true that the philosopher criticized some of the sayings of Jesus recorded in the Gospels, it is also true that for the first time he drew distinctions between the teachings and character of Jesus and those of his disciples. Not only is this attempt to distinguish the person of Jesus from the movement he inspired fascinating in its own right, but Jesus' elevation by an opponent has important implications for both our discussion of Christian exclusivism and Porphyry's rhetorical strategy.

Naturally, there are similarities as well as differences between Celsus' anti-Christian arguments and those of Porphyry. Since both critics shared the presuppositions of Platonic philosophy, both condemned the Christian teaching of the resurrection; although Porphyry attributed immortality to Jesus, such a status was based upon a personal eschatology of the disembodied soul in a blessed state, not a physical resurrection. In addition, both critics attacked the disciples of Jesus as presented in the New Testament, calling them simpletons or deceivers or both. Celsus and Porphyry both attributed to the Christians a reliance upon blind faith and intransigence when it came to listening to reason.

On the whole, however, the differences between Celsus and Porphyry are more apparent than their similarities. Some of these differences are a result of the improved position of Christianity by the second half of the third century. Others stem from a difference in emphasis between the two writers, especially Porphyry's concentration on New Testament inconsistencies. In addition, there is a nearly complete lack of philosophical sophistication on the part of Porphyry, whereas many of Celsus' arguments are buttressed by Platonic arguments.

As may be expected, their treatments of Christian exclusivism differed markedly as well. While it was noted previously that Celsus offered no organized philosophical resistance to exclusivism *per se*, he at least touched upon those social and theological aspects of exclusivism that he found offensive. Porphyry's objections to the idea are less explicit still. On the other hand, a few examples of his anti-Christian polemic will enable us to gain some insight into the state of the objection, especially when it is placed in the context of philosophical and political moves toward religious syncretism in the third century. The first specific element of Porphyry's critique discussed here has to do with Christianity's appearance in relatively recent time; if it is the only true religion, what happened to all the people who lived before the time of Jesus? The second element of interest is Porphyry's search for a "universal way" of salvation that would be applicable for all people at all times. Third, as we have briefly mentioned, Porphyry described Christ as having been pious as well as elevated to immortal status. We will observe their implications for our study as we treat each of these developments in turn.

One specific element of Christian teaching made the religion particularly vulnerable to objections against exclusivism. This characteristic was that its central myth occurred at a particular geographic location and at a specific time that could be dated through historical records. The incarnation of the Christian deity and his crucifixion and resurrection, according to Christian teaching, happened in Palestine during the reigns of Augustus and Tiberius. This assertion was susceptible to the question of why Christ came so late, thus depriving of salvation all the people who lived before him. How could Christians claim that their faith was universal when its very origin in time and space prevented people in some times and places from embracing it?

Thus the historical nature of the Christian myth exposed Christians to a particular criticism that Porphyry discussed at length in *Against the Christians*. The combination of historicity with exclusivism raised a difficult problem for Christian apologists: if salvation is through Christ alone, why was salvation not available to those who lived before his coming? The converse of this question posed an equal difficulty: if the God of the Christians intended salvation to be universal, why did he wait so long in history before sending Jesus to proclaim it and make it possible? It is just such a combination of historically limited revelation and an exclusive claim to salvation, especially when coupled with a cultural value that revered what was ancient and despised innovation, that placed a virtually unanswerable criticism in the armory of anti-Christian critics.

Porphyry was quite aware of the problem and capitalized upon it. One fragment of his argument, found in one of Augustine's epistles, summarizes the issue.

> If Christ says he is the way, the grace, and the truth, and He places in Himself alone the approach of believing souls to Him, what did the men of so many centuries before Christ do? . . . What, [Porphyry] says, became of the innumerable souls, who were entirely guiltless, if He, in whom they could believe had not yet lent His presence to men? The world, also, as well as Rome, was devoted to the religious rites of its temples. Why, he says, did He who is called the Savior, hide Himself for so many ages? But, he says, let them not say that the human race was saved by the ancient Jewish law, since the Jewish law appeared and flourished in a small part of Syria, a long time after, and still later made its way into the Italian lands, after the reign of Gaius Caesar, or probably during his reign. What, then, became of the souls of Romans or Latins who were deprived of the grace of Christ not yet come until the time of the Caesars?[15]

Besides the primary question of the lateness of Christ's coming, two other points in Porphyry's argument are relevant to our discussion. In the first place, he recognized that this problem could exist only in the context of Christian exclusivism: ". . .and He places in

Himself alone the approach of believing souls to Him." Other religions such as Mithraism and the cult of Isis were making claims to universality at the same time as Christianity; they were not, however, demanding exclusive allegiance. Only Christianity was saddled with the problem of explaining its deity's inaction to save people of former generations. Christianity's positive refusal to recognize either the worship of other gods or the efficacy of other ways of salvation—in other words, exclusivism—was not shared by the other universal religions. The question of why Jesus came so recently after so much human history had passed was, therefore, a refutation of the exclusive claims of Christians.

Second, Porphyry anticipated—or, more likely, responded to—the argument of Christian apologists that Judaism had been the ancient precursor to their religion. Christians had long asserted the legitimacy of their faith by arguing that it was in fact ancient and that they were the true heirs of the Jewish religion. In any event, an appeal to the antiquity of Judaism was unconvincing to Porphyry, since Judaism had the same problem as Christianity in that its origin was localized in space and time.

This particular objection to Christian exclusivism had plagued Christians for two centuries. While Porphyry's argument had been expressed before, a discussion of the Christian answer is of some relevance to our discussion. As early as the middle of the first century, Paul referred to the moral responsibility of those who did not have the Jewish law (Romans 2:14–15) as well as the problem of those who had lived from Adam to Moses (Romans 5:13–14). Pagan opponents seem to have raised the question as early as the the middle of the second century. Justin Martyr responded to pagans who complained that "we affirm that Christ was born one hundred and fifty years ago under Quirenius. . . and should accuse us as if [we said] all men born before the time of Christ were not accountable for their actions. . ." Justin's creative response was that there had been many "Christians" who lived before the time of Christ—as long as they had lived μετὰ λόγου, in accordance with the dictates of the universal Logos given to all humanity.[16]

In later writers, however, a curious contradiction can be detected in the Christian discussion of the origins of their faith. While most apologists were asserting the antiquity of Christianity,[17] others made no apology for the fact that Christ appeared during the reign of

Augustus at the beginning of the Roman Empire. Could the timing of Jesus' coming have been mere coincidence? Some Christians believed not. As early as the reign of Marcus Aurelius (161–180 CE) the bishop Melito of Sardis said as much to the emperor.

> The philosophy which we profess, first indeed, flourished among the barbarians, but afterwards, when it grew up, also among the nations under your government; under the glorious reign of Augustus your ancestor, it became, especially to your reign, an auspicious blessing. For since that time, the Roman power has grown in greatness and splendour. Whose desired successor you have become, and will be, together with your son, if you preserve that philosophy which has been nurtured with the empire, which commenced its existence with Augustus. . .[18]

Thus Christianity, according to Melito, was responsible for the prosperity of the empire. It is no accident that we find this fragment preserved by Eusebius of Caesarea, whose fourth-century political theology would echo and build significantly upon that of Melito.

Origen offered another reason for Christianity's appearance during the reign of Augustus. Instead of asserting that Christianity had brought peace to the empire, he theorized that God had brought peace to the empire in order to prepare the world for the propagation of the gospel. Later, Eusebius would also speculate that God had arranged the uniting of the world under Augustus for the furtherance of the gospel; it was no coincidence that "[Jesus'] wonderful sojourn among men synchronized with Rome's attainment of the acme of power."[19] At this earlier date (between 314 and 318 for his *Proof of the Gospel* just quoted) in Eusebius' career, however, his political theology had not yet been developed. With his *Life of Constantine* would come the more explicit political theology of the Roman state in which Christianity and Empire were one; it would be God himself who had appointed Constantine sole ruler of the empire. The connection between the emperor's faith and his rule over the world would become explicit, as Constantine "was the first to proclaim to all the sole sovereignty of God, so he himself, as sole sovereign of the Roman world, extended his authority over the whole human race."[20]

In 270, however, Eusebius' political theory was still in the future. On the other hand, a Christian view of the relationship between

Christianity and the Roman state had been developing since Melito in the second century, and in Porphyry's own lifetime Origen had articulated his apologetic for the simultaneous birth of church and empire. It is uncertain whether Porphyry had read any of the relevant works of Origen, or specifically whether he was aware of this particular apologetic. That he indeed knew of at least some Christian responses to the criticism is clear from his protest against the argument that salvation had come through Judaism in a more distant past than the coming of Christ. But the Christians' argument that would become the foundation of the Byzantine state, namely the convergence of church and empire, was developing apparently unnoticed by their pagan opponents. As an argument against Christian exclusivism, Porphyry's objection to the late coming of Christ was logically coherent. However, it was largely a repetition of anti-Christian argument from the second and perhaps even the first centuries; the Christian response, on the other hand, was proceeding inexorably into the fourth century, into the political exclusivism of Constantine and his successors.

Porphyry's objection had been advanced for over a century: that the appearance of the Christian faith in recent time and literal space rendered illogical its claims to universal theological exclusivism. Did such an objection, however, preclude the very possibility of a single and universally valid way of salvation? Could there be, even if Christianity was not the vehicle to provide it, a system of religious cult or philosophical wisdom that transcended the boundaries of nationality and localized cultic practice? This question and Porphyry's answer to it impinge directly upon the critique of universalist Christianity. Porphyry's interaction with Christian exclusivism would be informed in large measure, as it was for Celsus, by the polemicist's view of the ultimate nature of religion, particularly the ultimate unity of otherwise diverse religious beliefs and practices.

It is clear that at some point in his career Porphyry answered affirmatively the question of a universal way of salvation, applicable to all peoples and times. According to Augustine, in whose works many of Porphyry's fragments are found, Porphyry was certain that such a way existed, although its particulars were as yet unknown:

Now Porphyry says—towards the end of his first book *On the Return of the Soul*—that no doctrine has yet been established to form the teaching of a philosophical sect, which offers a universal way for the liberation of the soul; no such way has been produced by any philosophy (in the truest sense of the word), or by the moral teaching and disciplines of the Indians, or by the magical spells of the Chaldeans, or in any other way, and that this universal way had never been brought to his knowledge in his study of history. He admits without any doubt that such a way exists, but confesses that it had never come to his notice.[21]

Assuming the veracity of Augustine's (admittedly hostile) report of Porphyry's writing, the result of Porphyry's own search for a universal salvation led to two conclusions. In the first place, such a system had never been synthesized. That is, a universally valid way of salvation was not to be found in any of the currently existing philosophical systems or religious cults, no matter how ancient or sophisticated; nor would conventional polytheism in itself qualify. Second, he was positive that such a way nevertheless existed, even if it could not currently be identified.

It may be asked how he conceived of such a universalism. Since it did not exist in the form of any of the available cults or philosophies, whether national or local, what kind of "existence" did this universal way have for Porphyry if it had never been found? We are not particularly assisted by the final point of Augustine's account, namely that Porphyry himself, although he believed that a person could be mystically united with the One (and even claimed to have attained such a union once, at the age of sixty-eight[22]), believed that although such a way existed, he had never discovered it. If he had once found individual "liberation," how could he say that he had not found a universal way? That is, if Porphyry experienced "salvation," how could he claim that he had not found "a universal way for the liberation of the soul"? Even if Porphyry wrote *On the Return of the Soul* before his own experience of union, his master Plotinus' experience would have informed him that salvation was indeed possible. Unfortunately, his own statement on the subject is limited; more context is required. Thus to make any attempt to understand his belief it will be necessary briefly to summarize Platonic theology as it had developed by the time of Porphyry.

Plato's theory of the Forms or Ideas postulated a "world" of unseen entities beyond the realm of sense perception, entities that gave unity and meaning to the physical world. Chief among the Forms was the Form of the Good, the ultimate principle and the source of all the other Forms. A later period of philosophical reflection commonly known as Middle Platonism (from the first century BCE to the third century CE) is not easily described, since no singular interpretation of Plato prevailed.[23] What was more or less common among the Middle Platonists was the concept of the Forms belonging to a metaphysical hierarchy and as thoughts of the Good.[24]

Neoplatonism, a system of Platonic interpretation fathered by Plotinus (204–270 CE), made several crucial moves with regard to the ultimate principle. First, the One was ultimately transcendent, radically separate from the Middle Platonic hierarchy of being. In addition Plotinus ascribed a radical simplicity to the One, beyond even the simplicity of numerical unity. This simplicity of ultimate reality was related to its transcendence; it was distinct from all else in that it did not partake of the complexity that was inherent in the lower levels of reality.[25] Finally, the One was not apprehended ultimately by the intellect, but rather by mystical experience. While classical Platonism had stressed knowledge of the divine in terms of dialectic reasoning, Plotinus believed that a mystical union with the One was a necessary step subsequent to apprehension by philosophical reasoning.[26]

Porphyry, too, believed in the mystical union, reporting that he himself had attained it once. On the other hand, it must be remembered that he was no philosophical elitist. He was a religious man who sincerely believed in traditional forms of religious expression; his work *Philosophy from Oracles* was, after all, an attempt to reconcile Platonic philosophy with what he considered to be the best of the popular religious tradition. It would seem probable that it was just such a combination of religious and philosophical interests that influenced Porphyry to postulate a universal system including, but not restricted to, the Neoplatonic mystical union.

So we are left with the question: in what terms did Porphyry conceive of a "universal way for the liberation of the soul"? As mentioned earlier, he denied that such a way existed in any known philosophical sect or in any religious tradition, nor had it ever existed in such a form. However, Porphyry seems to have affirmed his belief "without any doubt that such a way exists." And indeed, the fact that Plotinus (and later, Porphyry himself) had experienced mystical union was enough evidence for him that the potential for individual salvation actually existed.

The contradiction between Porphyry's belief in the existence of a true universalism and his observation that such a universalism did not exist in any known form is real enough; unfortunately, our direct knowledge of Porphyry's universalism is limited. From Augustine's description, it seems to have been primarily apophatic in nature; we know what it was not, but little regarding what it was. This observation, plus the fragmentary state of the evidence and the fact that our knowledge of it comes primarily from Augustine, his later Christian opponent, renders our understanding of Porphyry problematic on this issue. We are assisted by a general understanding of some of his concerns, namely a desire to preserve traditional religion, as well as a commitment to the Neoplatonic metaphysics of Plotinus.

With this in mind, we may nonetheless cautiously and tentatively characterize Porphyry's "universalism" as an undiscovered theoretical construct whose object was the transcendent One that was beyond being and beyond the predication of attributes. Although this universalism provided "liberation" for the individual, perhaps in the form of the mystical experience enjoyed by adepts such as Plotinus, it transcended known philosophical categories; otherwise, the experience as he understood it would itself have constituted the "universal way." It is the very universalism of his understanding that is most problematic; if it was not subsumed under the teachings of Platonic philosophy and the interpretations of Plotinus in particular, what could possibly have provided the framework for such a system?

Perhaps the key is to be found in Porphyry's sympathy with traditional religious practice. Recall that Porphyry attempted to reconcile popular religion, in particular the respected oracles of the Mediterranean world, to Neoplatonic philosophy. Such a reconciliation of interests suggests that his enthusiasm for the unity of traditional religion and philosophy constituted at least one significant element of his "universal way." Philosophy alone, including the mystical union as Porphyry understood it, may have been too restricted to the elite for him to consider it truly universal, while on the other hand the traditional religious practices of the nations were too diffuse and varied to qualify. It is possible that Porphyry's idea of universal salvation included the best elements of the realms of both philosophy and religion. While the specifics—if Porphyry ever articulated any—must remain unknown to us, it is likely in any event that the universalism of which he was so certain "existed" only as an ideal, an ideal he never realized.

Porphyry's belief in the existence of a true universalism was similar in some respects to that of Celsus. There was, however, an important difference between the understandings of the two critics. Celsus' universal way was, practically speaking, merely an extension of polytheism, of the national and local religious diversity that currently existed. By worshiping the gods, Celsus asserted, one worshiped the supreme deity. And even if such a God were to be specifically worshiped, he would in reality be nothing more than the supreme deity of each of the nations—Zeus, Jupiter, and so forth. Porphyry, on the other hand, believed that a particular universal religious system actually existed, or at least had the potential to exist, above and beyond (but perhaps including) known religious expression. No one of the variety of current religious beliefs served the purpose. Unlike Celsus, Porphyry did not settle upon the eclectic acceptance of all forms of worship as valid and as ultimately serving the supreme deity.

The difference between the two writers on this issue is important. Celsus' theory of a universal religion was in reality nothing more than a defense of conventional polytheism; no pagan who accepted Celsus' universalism would have had to change anything about the way he or she honored the gods. In other words, the realization that the worship of the gods ultimately benefited the supreme deity would have been nothing more than that—a simple realization. Porphyry, on the other hand, took seriously the problem that a universally valid religious system might actually exist *outside* the variety of religious expression available in the third century, beyond either a theoretical implication of conventional polytheism or in the religious traditions of other nations. As much as Porphyry was a proponent of traditional religious expression, when it came to a universal religion he was a seeker, not a defender of existing religion as was Celsus.

From Celsus to Porphyry, then, we observe a significant shift away from a universalism based upon existing cultic and philosophical variety and toward a true universalism that transcended local variations in belief and practice. However, whether and how much this difference is a reflection of an actual trend over the course of the third century is difficult to determine based only upon the writings of the two critics. Was Porphyry merely an important exception to an otherwise relatively unchanged religious scene, or were there other measurable developments of which Porphyry's universalism was a symptom? To what degree is the change detectable during this period in other venues such as popular religious belief and imperial cult?

As it happens, there is evidence that the universalizing trend detected from Celsus to Porphyry was indeed evident in other areas. On the level of imperial religious policy, this trend reached a watershed about the same time that Porphyry was writing *Against the Christians*. As we have mentioned briefly, the emperor Aurelian, in the process of restoring the empire from the perilous conditions prevalent in the middle of the third century, made an attempt to unify religious belief throughout the Roman world. In 274 the emperor built a temple to the sun god *Sol Invictus* in Rome, and the Senate declared the deity the official god of the empire.[27] Significantly, the statues of other gods were brought into the new temple, symbolizing the supreme and syncretistic nature of the cult of Sol. In addition, such a religion had the virtue of being independent of the cult of the emperor; "It probably seemed decreasingly meaningful to offer divine honors to the ephemeral rulers spawned by the crisis of the mid-third century."[28] Even if individual emperors should come and go, *Sol Invictus* would remain.

In light of the near-disintegration of the empire, Aurelian's religious reform was an attempt to facilitate recovery by re-establishing some form of identity for the broken empire. Sun-worship was already popular in the east and had also become popular among the army; Aurelian took steps to ensure that the new cult would also be acceptable to Roman sensibilities. Having achieved political and territorial unity, he now sought to establish religious unity as well. Aurelian's solar cult had religious precursors; a temple of the Sun had existed in Rome since at least the late republic. Elagabalus (218–222), the young emperor from Emesa who was the hereditary priest of the Syrian sun-god, had made an earlier attempt to elevate this deity to supremacy over all other Roman gods. Though his efforts shocked the Romans and the emperor was killed as a result, Aurelian's efforts would be accepted fifty years later.

Of course, "syncretism" was not a phenomenon limited to the third century CE. The Roman Jupiter and the Greek Zeus had been identified with each other centuries before, as had Poseidon and Neptune, Mercury and Hermes, and a host of other greater and lesser gods of Greece and Rome as well as other nations. In many ways, the syncretism we are observing from the Isis of Plutarch and Apuleius to the cult of *Sol Invictus* was a continuation of a centuries-long process of such integration. Thus Porphyry's search for a unifying soteriology was only one manifestation of an ongoing phenomenon with religious, political and philosophical dimensions. "Foreign" religions had already been openly embraced by the Semitic Severan dynasty in the early third century. In 212 the emperor Caracalla had declared virtually all free males to be Roman citizens; this move was perhaps the first widely visible sign of a unifying process that would gain inertia through the third century. Aurelian's institution of the cult of *Sol Invictus* as a universal religion was "an important stage in the prehistory of the Christian doctrine of empire forged by Constantine and formulated by Eusebius: one god, one empire, one emperor."[29]

This discussion has attempted to establish a philosophical and religious context for the pagan treatment of Christian exclusivism in the latter half of the third century. Porphyry's search for a unifying religious system, in addition to the actual establishment of an empire-wide solar cult, serve as indicators of the syncretistic tendencies operating in the decade of the 270s.

These tendencies had consequences for the opposition to Christianity. Specifically, they allowed pagans to look at some aspects of the Christian religion in a manner that would have been impossible at the time Celsus wrote his *True Doctrine*. Things had changed since the turn of the century. The growing acceptability of foreign religions and Aurelian's solar cult constituted some of the more visible manifestations of these changes. For Porphyry the anti-Christian polemicist, even Christianity could in some small way be accommodated in this environment. According to Augustine, such accommodation took the form of allowing Christ a status greater than the "sorcerer" of Celsus' polemic:

What I am going to say may certainly appear startling to some. I mean the fact that the gods have pronounced Christ to have been extremely devout, and have said that he has become immortal, and that they mention him in terms of commendation; whereas the Christians, by their account, are polluted and contaminated and entangled in error; and there are many other such slanders they issue against them.[30]

Quick as the critic was to distinguish the "contamination" of the followers of Christ from the piety of Christ himself, Porphyry nonetheless made a critical move. Up to this time, Jesus had been roundly condemned as a magician and a deceiver; Justin had alluded to such accusations even before Celsus. Porphyry's approach of honoring Jesus as an "extremely devout" immortal, on the other hand, reveals the lengths to which he was willing to go in order to incorporate all forms of religious belief. If indeed Jesus' commendation was uttered by a respected oracle, then the shift was not Porphyry's alone; it was also occurring elsewhere in the religious universe.

Such willingness to pronounce Christ devout was in no way a capitulation to the Christians. On the contrary, the commendation of Jesus fell squarely within the bounds of Græco-Roman religious tradition; the oracle did not accept the immortality of Jesus on Christian terms. In the first place, Porphyry's exaltation of Jesus was a tacit denial of Christ's bodily resurrection; belief in immortality among the Greeks was generally limited to the continuing existence after death of the disembodied soul.[31] As we will see, the oracle of Hecate emphasized the separation of Jesus' soul from his body; while the utterance did not directly refute the Christian doctrine of physical resurrection, the implication was clear.

In addition, the utterance of the oracle stood firmly within a centuries-old Greek tradition. Oracular declarations, particularly those of the oracle at Delphi, were often, although not always, a prerequisite for elevating a deceased human being to immortal status.[32] People so honored were usually regarded as "heroes," not as a technical designation, but because in the earliest form of the practice those who were thus honored had served their *polis* in a special way, either as a lawgiver or in a military capacity. People were later immortalized for other reasons, such as outstanding virtue or piety; Roman emperors (except for those whose memories were posthumously condemned) routinely received deification after their deaths.

Other people were sometimes honored for their special relationship to a god, such as Sophocles, who introduced the worship of Asclepius to Athens.

Thus the pronouncement of immortal status upon Jesus for being "extremely devout" was not in itself unusual, especially since it was given on oracular authority. In fact, such authority may be considered an attempt by Porphyry to claim the traditional right of the oracles to pronounce immortality, in direct opposition to the authority claimed by Christians for their scriptures. In this way, having secured the proper traditional authority for immortality, Jesus could be "domesticated" for pagan veneration. If Jesus was going to be included in the realm of the blessed, it would be on pagan terms.

Thus Porphyry granted Jesus the status of a hero while at the same time condemning the Christians as "polluted and contaminated and entangled in error." This condemnation of the Christians is significant. If he was willing to move toward the acceptance of Jesus as a pious immortal, why did he single out Jesus' followers for criticism? Part of the answer lies in the fact that they considered him not merely a pious man, but as God.

> On the other hand, to those who asked whether Christ was God, Hecate replied, "You know that the immortal soul goes on its way after it leaves the body; whereas when it is cut off from wisdom it wanders for ever. That soul [of Jesus] belongs to a man of outstanding piety; this they worship because truth is a stranger to them."[33]

The oracle of Hecate did not stop here. It was necessary, if one was to assign Jesus a place among the immortals, to explain the relationship between him and his followers. To this end the oracle described the place of Christians in the divinely ordered universe.

> Thus Hecate said that [Jesus] was a most devout man, and that his soul, like the souls of other devout men, was endowed after death with the immortality it deserved; and that the Christians in their ignorance worship this soul. . . . That is why they were hated by the gods, because, not being fated to know God or to receive gifts from the gods, they were given by this man the fatal gift of entanglement in error. For all that, he himself was devout, and, like other devout men, passed into heaven. And so you shall not slander him, but pity the insanity of men. From him comes for them a ready peril of headlong disaster. . . .

Uninstructed and ungodly natures, however, to which fate has not granted the gifts of the gods and the knowledge of immortal Jupiter, have not listened to the gods and to inspired men; and so they have rejected all the gods. . .[34]

The exclusive nature of their worship was the true cause of the Christians' "insanity," and the "insane" Christians had received the "gift" of error from the gods. Their god Jesus, while himself devout, presided nonetheless over a divinely categorized company of fools. The Christians themselves were no longer divorced from theological reality as they had been in Celsus' totalizing discourse, but were now assigned a place, no matter how abhorrent their beliefs, within the religious cosmos.

Significantly, Christianity was now, in a limited and theoretical way at least, integrated into Porphyry's religious understanding. To be sure, he still regarded Christians as ignorant and impious; their beliefs were still objectionable, their rejection of the gods intolerable and worthy of punishment. Their presence, however, had come to be accepted as an irreversible fact of life; their exclusivism, as objectionable as it remained, was accepted as well. Not that this characteristic of Christianity was at all "acceptable" in any way; Porphyry still referred to their rejection of the gods as erroneous and insane. Only now, Christian "insanity" in the form of religious exclusivism had achieved its own theological standing.

Dramatic changes had occurred between the writing of the *True Doctrine* of Celsus and the critique of Porphyry. For the empire, the golden age of the Severi had succumbed to two generations of chaos. The church, meanwhile, had experienced steady growth in both numbers and respectability, the persecution of Decius notwithstanding. By the year 270 Christianity had become a permanent and powerful presence in the Mediterranean world. Having grown in numbers, organization and philosophical sophistication, the church was no longer in a precarious position with its survival on the line.

As a result of the staying power and growth of Christianity, pagan critics faced a curious situation, namely, how to integrate a persistent exclusive universalism into the "pluralistic" religious life of the empire. Porphyry's (and the oracles') bestowal of immortal status upon Jesus was wholly in step with the spirit of the middle to late third century. It also represented a resignation to the permanence of the church. Earlier, Celsus had expressed the desire that Christians would somehow return to their senses; Porphyry entertained no such hope. According to Porphyry, in agreement with Celsus, Christians were certainly deluded. Only now, Christian "delusion" was a permanent part of the religious landscape.

How could the person of Jesus have been made acceptable to Porphyry's oracles? Even though Jesus was condemned, according to Porphyry, by "right-thinking judges," he found a place nonetheless in the critic's hall of pious immortals. Thus a significant change took place between Celsus' and Porphyry's descriptions of Christ. To Celsus, Jesus had been nothing more than a deceiver and a magician. Of course, not everything Porphyry said about Jesus was positive either. He complained that Jesus seemed ignorant of physical digestive processes in Matthew 15:17ff. Porphyry also pointed out that, in John 7, Jesus went to the Feast of Tabernacles after telling his brothers that he would be staying home. On the other hand, Porphyry's accusations of an occasionally ignorant or fickle Jesus were relatively tame compared with Celsus' portrayal of Christ. What could be the explanation of this shift toward a relative tolerance of Christ, though not of Christians?

For Porphyry, it appears that his favorable regard of Christ was a result of his own desire to assimilate as many elements of existing religious belief as possible into his philosophy. Early in his career, at least, Porphyry believed the Jewish God to have been a powerful deity who governed the created universe as well as other gods. His *Philosophy from Oracles* reports an oracle of Apollo that declared,

in God, the begetter and the king before all things, at whom heaven trembles, and earth and sea and the hidden depths of the underworld and the very divinities shudder in dread; their law is the Father whom the holy Hebrews greatly honour.[35]

Judaism and the Jewish deity had come into favor at last. This seems to have been as true for the Severan dynasty in the opening decades of the third century as it was for Porphyry, if the *Augustan History* can be trusted regarding the pro-Jewish leanings of the Severans. "Foreign" religions were no longer the threat they once posed. Likewise, Porphyry's oracles concerning Jesus may reflect a growing tolerance of the Jewish elements of Christianity.

For those who followed Christ, however, Porphyry had no sympathy. Jesus served only as a "patron saint of fools"; Christians were, as far as Porphyry was concerned, cut off entirely from the piety that characterized the immortalized Jesus. Augustine's interpretation of this move was probably close to the mark when he observed that the oracles' praise of Christ was an aid, not an obstacle, to Porphyry's criticism of Christians, and that

> Their intention is that when a man has believed both praise and slander
> they may turn him into an admirer of Christ, but an admirer who has no
> wish to become a Christian. . . one who acknowledges Christ only as a
> man, not as God also.[36]

If Augustine's interpretation of Porphyry is correct—and there is little reason to reject his conclusion, given what we know from Porphyry's own statements—a good pagan could admire Christ without converting to Christianity, and certainly without worshiping him as the supreme God. Such an attitude of acceptance was a repudiation of the Christian idea that other gods were not worthy of worship. Porphyry's assertion that it should be possible to admire Christ and not become a Christian was essentially an argument against Christian exclusivism; by including Christ in the company of the immortals, Porphyry made the ingenious move of promoting Jesus from the low esteem in which he had previously been held while simultaneously barring him from exclusive status. While it would eventually fail, his experiment with a non-exclusive Christianity marks an important step in the pagan polemic against Christian exclusivism.

It is also an indicator of the gradual convergence between Christian belief and what pagans were now able to find acceptable. The fact that a traditional pagan oracle affirmed the piety and immortality of Jesus a mere two decades after the Decian persecution is no small development. Other ideas that Porphyry expressed in his polemic also point to convergences in the pagan-Christian universe. His universalistic beliefs, in whatever specific ways he may have actually held them, were not at all foreign to Christian thinkers. Even some Christians admitted the possibility of salvation outside of the Christian gospel in the context of explaining the fate of those who lived before Christ. Although Christianity was nowhere to be found within pagan religon, it was to be found in Plato. At least some aspects of Christian doctrine were thus "universal" in the sense that they were available outside of the special revelation of the gospel.

Other convergences can also be detected in the pagan-Christian interchange of this period. In the context of Porphyry's objection and the apologetic response regarding the question of Christ's late appearance, we found Christians arguing that the coming of Jesus during the reign of Augustus was fortunate for both the empire and the faith. By connecting the welfare of the state with the correct form of worship, Christians shared more in common with persecutors such as Decius and with their polemic opponents than they perhaps realized. Finally, we have mentioned Porphyry's passion to unite both Platonic philosophy and popular religion into a coherent system; such was also the desire of Christian philosophers from Justin to Origen and beyond. Christianity would eventually claim the process of union, as well as the philosophical tradition on which it rested, as its own. It was a claim that Julian would resist vehemently.

From Celsus to Porphyry, the issue of social exclusivism had disappeared; Christians had become as fully integrated as their rejection of the gods would allow. At the same time, the religious syncretism of the Severi and, later, of Aurelian provided a markedly different context for Christianity than had existed at the time of Celsus. Political and philosophical trends were moving in the direction of universalism and syncretism; Porphyry's own quest for a single religious solution paralleled Aurelian's universalizing cult of *Sol Invictus.*

Both the new syncretistic environment and the growing influence of the Christian church demanded new strategies in anti-Christian polemic. The genius of Porphyry's approach was his attempt at limited assimilation. Could Christ, if not the religion he inspired, be presented as a member of the larger family of Mediterranean belief systems? Porphyry seems to have believed so. His legitimation of Jesus added an element of acceptability to Christianity that would not have been possible a hundred years earlier. Such legitimation represents a shift over the course of the third century from Celsus' totalizing discourse of exclusion to a more flexible rhetoric of assimilation. However, it is important to understand that this shift represents not an acceptance of Christian exclusivism (or even of Christianity) but rather another way of rejecting it. His tactic differed from that of Celsus by drawing the boundary, not so much between Christianity and paganism, but between Christianity and Christ. This movement of the rhetorical boundaries, necessitated by both the success of the church and universalizing tendencies within paganism, would be continued in new and perhaps more important ways by the last pagan emperor.

5

Julian the Apostate and the Politics of Hellenism

Of our anti-Christian polemicists thus far, Celsus is unknown to us other than as the author of the *True Doctrine*, while Porphyry was a philosopher from the Neoplatonic school of Plotinus. With the emperor Julian (331/2–363 CE), tagged by early Christian historians as "the Apostate" and the last pagan ruler of the Roman Empire, we encounter not only the final important critic of Christianity, but perhaps the most fascinating personality of late antiquity.[1] That our final critic was the last pagan emperor gives us a unique perspective not only into the development of anti-Christian polemic but also into the last decades of pagan power before its own marginalization, at least as a political force, by Christianity toward the end of the fourth century.

The facts of Julian's life are well known from his own writings as well as those of several historians of the period. The son of Constantine's half brother, Julian was five years old when Constantine died in 337. A few months after the emperor's death a purge of many members of Constantine's family, likely initiated by his oldest son Constantius, reduced the chances of an immediate political challenge to the sons of Constantine. Julian's father was killed, as well as at least eight other members of the imperial family; Julian was spared on account of his youth. That Julian later blamed Constantius for the murder of his family is plain enough from his later writings.[2]

Julian spent his boyhood in relatively luxurious exile. During his education he learned to appreciate the Greek classics as well as Christian texts, an appreciation that would later translate into legislation when as emperor he prohibited Christians from teaching the classics. While the date of his "conversion" to paganism has been debated, Julian's own writings seem to point to a date of 350 or 351. In any event, he concealed his pagan leanings for several years, except in the presence of a few close pagan friends. Outwardly, however, he continued to practice Christianity; only later, after he was made Augustus, did he dare proclaim his paganism openly.

In 355 Constantius, engaged in the East against the Persians, appointed Julian as Caesar and sent him to Gaul to counter the growing barbarian incursions there. Julian's successes won him favor with the soldiers; when, in early 360, Constantius ordered some of Julian's troops to march east to augment his Persian campaign, the soldiers revolted against the order. Instead they proclaimed Julian as Augustus in Paris.[3] While Julian led his army eastward for a final confrontation with his cousin, Constantius died of natural causes. Civil war thus averted, Julian entered Constantinople unopposed in December 361. By that time he had publicly declared his allegiance to paganism, having openly performed pagan sacrifice on his march to the capital.

> I worship the gods openly, and the whole mass of the troops who are returning with me worship the gods. . . . The gods command me to restore their worship in its utmost purity, and I obey them, yes, and with a good will.[4]

Julian remained in the capital for only six months, then moved eastward once again to continue the still-pressing Persian war. He wintered in Syrian Antioch, during which time he managed on a number of counts to incur the contempt of the primarily Christian citizens of that city. His attempts to alleviate a food shortage there merely exacerbated the problem, while his attempts to restore pagan cult were met with indifference even among the pagan population. In the spring of 363 he marched toward the Persian capital; after initially overcoming strong resistance, his army failed to take the city. On June 26, 363, during the retreat out of Mesopotamia, Julian was struck down by an enemy spear and died during the night. The leaderless troops elevated a Christian soldier named Jovian to the rank of Augustus, thus ending pagan rule.

Like Celsus and Porphyry, Julian wrote an anti-Christian treatise, entitled *Against the Galileans,* its substance preserved in a fifth-century refutation by Cyril of Alexandria. Naturally, appearing as they did after three centuries of pagan-Christian conflict, some of Julian's arguments against Christianity built upon those we have already encountered. Although many have compared his polemic work with those of Celsus and Porphyry, the detailed comparison remains to be written; scholars have noted generally and correctly that while Julian probably used some of the material from Porphyry's *Against the Christians*, the tone of his attack harkens back to Celsus' *True Doctrine*.[5] While it is true that Julian did use some of the earlier arguments, a closer examination reveals that he significantly shifted their focus and expanded them to serve a purpose not envisioned (or at least not articulated) by either Celsus or Porphyry.

While Julian's arguments were in many cases similar, their ideological motivations and specific lines of reasoning underwent substantial development since their introduction by the earlier polemicists. It is argued in this and the following chapter that Julian's contributions to these older arguments reveal the primary theme of *Against the Galileans* and of his anti-Christian program generally. Although the polemic is an anti-Christian literary work in the tradition of Celsus and Porphyry, its main thrust was an apologetic for traditional Hellenistic culture, termed here the "Hellenistic apology."

That Julian was an apologist for Hellenism is not a matter of controversy. In particular, the work of Polymnia Athanassiadi-Fowden on Julian's Hellenism has highlighted the emperor's ideology and motivations. What is less understood, however, is the relationship between his ideology and his anti-Christian polemic. Athanassiadi-Fowden's insight[6] that *Against the Galileans* was the clearest declaration of Julian's Hellenistic ideal requires further demonstration and discussion; the comparison of Julian's critique of Christianity with those of Celsus and Porphyry still carries the momentum in the study of his polemic work. This present study synthesizes further these two aspects of the study of Julian. In addition, as we will see, Julian's Hellenistic apology was directed in large measure against the Christian appropriation of Hellenism; an examination of Julian's agenda displays the open confrontation between pagans and Christians over the cultural and intellectual property of the Roman Empire—a conflict every bit as important as their struggle for political power.

A further aspect of Julian's work concerns elements of the objection to Christian exclusivism. Some of these elements, identified in previous chapters and modified by Julian, form the framework, if not the basis, of Julian's Hellenistic apology. Finally, it is argued that Julian's approach, like Porphyry's, was largely a rhetoric of assimilation. As similar as Julian's tone and content are to those of Celsus, *Against the Galileans* employed a strategy of marginalization closer to that of Porphyry.

Before proceeding it will be necessary to place the life and reign of Julian in a broader historical context. Nearly a century passed between Porphyry's *Against the Christians* and the time of Julian's ascent to the throne; during this period enormous changes swept both church and empire. Christianity endured the Great Persecution at the turn of the fourth century and passed from an illegal religion to, with the help of the first Christian emperor Constantine and his successors, the official religion of the Roman Empire.

The decade after the emperor Aurelian's assassination in 275 CE failed to produce a stable mechanism either for identifying candidates for the purple or for the imperial succession. Diocletian, who rose to power in 284, initiated an innovative attempt to provide both. His plan was to appoint an Augustus junior to himself with whom he would share the responsibility of rule. Each Augustus would be assisted by an appointed Caesar, an arrangement that would effectively divide the management of the empire into four parts and provide for succession when an Augustus died. The First Tetrarchy consisted of Diocletian and Maximian as Augusti in east and west respectively, while their respective Caesars were Galerius and Constantius Chlorus. In an unprecedented move, possibly designed to test the stability of the system, the two Augusti abdicated in 305. Their juniors were raised to the rank of Augustus, while two new Caesars were appointed, Maximin Daia in the East and Severus in the West, thus constituting the Second Tetrarchy.

The tetrarchic system was in theory based on individual merit, independent of the uncertainties of birth and the whim of the army, and was intended to bring stability to the often chaotic conditions surrounding the death of a ruler. However, the system failed to quell the dynastic ambitions of Maxentius, the son of Maximian, and Constantine, the son of Constantius Chlorus. The crisis fueled by these ambitions was precipitated only a year after the institution of the Second Tetrarchy. Upon Constantius' death in 306 the soldiers in Britain hailed Constantine as Augustus, bothering neither with the lower office of Caesar nor with the constitutional rights of Severus, the legitimate Caesar in the West. Not to be outdone, Maxentius had himself proclaimed Augustus, while Severus likewise received promotion. The resulting civil wars introduced an era of instability reminiscent of the middle of the third century. Less than fifteen years after its inception, the system of the tetrarchy was dead. The experiment had failed.

At the same time, the early fourth century saw a renewal of the persecution of Christians, often called the "Great Persecution." Diocletian[7] initiated the action by issuing a series of anti-Christian decrees in 303 and 304. The first was limited to the removal of the privileges of high-ranking Christians and to the destruction of church buildings and scriptures; with the final edict all Christians were required to offer sacrifices to the gods. Although a large number of Christians were maimed and killed, many capitulated. The persecution continued until 311 when, just before his death, Galerius issued an edict of tolerance. After only six months' respite, however, his successor Maximinus in late 311 renewed the persecution.

Meanwhile in the West, Constantine consolidated his power. Maximian had come out of retirement to join his son Maxentius, eliminating Severus in 307. Galerius appointed his comrade Licinius as Augustus in the Balkans. Constantine eliminated Maxentius in 312; his victory was significant in that it served as the occasion for Constantine's embrace of Christianity. The night before meeting Maxentius in battle Constantine had a dream (or saw a vision[8]) instructing him to place the *chi-rho* monogram on his soldiers' shields, symbolizing the protection of the Christian God. After obeying what he considered to be a sign from God, he defeated Maxentius at the Milvian Bridge outside Rome. Over the next six years a series of civil wars eliminated all but Constantine in the West and Licinius in the East. Only six years after the dissolution of the Tetrarchy, Constantine was sole ruler in the West.

Shortly afterward, Constantine and Licinius issued a joint statement guaranteeing to everyone the freedom of worship, effectively ending the persecution of Christians in their domains. Maximinus in the East, just prior to his own defeat by Licinius, had issued a decree of toleration for Christians, perhaps in an attempt to win the favor of the same God who had helped Constantine. The Great Persecution was over, and the empire was divided between Licinius and Constantine. Eventually, however, the two Augusti came to blows, and in 324 Constantine defeated Licinius at Chrysopolis near the Bosporus. Constantine remianed in power until his death in 337, the first sole ruler of the Roman Empire since Diocletian instituted the Tetrarchy.

In the decades following Constantine's victory at the Milvian Bridge, Christianity moved from persecution to toleration, then eventually became the official religion of the state. It was in this environment that Julian was born and raised, as the balance of power shifted from paganism to the church. Thus an understanding of the five decades from Constantine's dream to Julian's accession are crucial to any investigation of the emperor Julian. In order to evaluate his criticism of Christianity adequately, it is necessary to trace the relationship between Christians and pagans over the course of the fourth century. It was only a lifetime between Constantine's victory in 312 and the edict of Theodosius I in 380 outlawing all forms of pagan worship, public and private. The reigns of Constantine and his sons, particularly Constantius, provide key landmarks in the development of the Christian state that Julian was ultimately powerless to prevent.

Constantine's victory over Maxentius was only the beginning of a process that would bring Christianity into a position of political and cultural dominance over the course of the fourth century. Much ink has been spilled tracing the development of the emperor's personal religious beliefs in an attempt to determine the relationship between his faith and his policies.[9] Our interest here, however, is not to try to examine the emperor's "sincerity" as a Christian, but rather to survey those aspects of his reign that give us insight into the official or "visible" elements of transition from a pagan to a Christian society.

Some of these elements were immediate. The newly Christian emperor favored Christianity with tax exemptions and grants for the repair and construction of churches. He gave jurisdiction to bishops for some types of court cases such as the manumission of slaves. Legal charges against bishops were not to be tried before secular courts but rather by the church. Bishops travelling to and from church councils were allowed to use the public post, the system of official transportation normally reserved for imperial business. In some respects Constantine was doing nothing new by granting these privileges; as *pontifex maximus*, or high priest, Roman emperors since Augustus had exercised such rights in matters of religion.[10]

Other aspects of Constantine's Christian policies indicate a gradual improvement of Christianity's status from the time of his victory over Maxentius. Some of the best evidence comes to us through his coinage. Pagan symbols continued to be represented, *Sol Invictus* in particular, at least until 321, a full decade after his embrace of Christianity.[11] This continuation of *Sol* indicates either that Constantine did not know that the Christian God was to be worshiped exclusively, or that he was familiar with the exclusivism of Christianity but was reluctant to alienate the pagan majority in order to placate a minority religion. The latter is more likely. It is highly improbable that any informed person could have been ignorant of Christian exclusivism, the one characteristic that set it apart from pagan religion.[12] The numismatic evidence, while indicating a gradual decline in the use of pagan inscriptions, suggests a period characterized by an official policy of co-existence for pagan and Christian in Constantine's imperial symbolism.

This co-existence was also visible in a number of other venues. For example, pagans as well as the Christian historian Eusebius were present at Constantine's court. The panegyric that a pagan orator delivered on behalf of Constantine after the defeat of Maxentius[13] named the gods not at all; over two decades later, Eusebius in his *Tricennial Oration* failed to name Christ.[14] The speeches were ambiguous enough regarding the identity of the deity to satisfy both (or, more likely, neither) Christians and pagans.

One of the more important pieces of evidence for the ambiguity of Constantine's religious policy consists of the accounts of the building and dedication of the new capital at Byzantium, which he renamed Constantinople.[15] Although his moving of the capital has been viewed[16] as an opportunity for him to create a Christian political center independent of the ensconced paganism of Rome, Constantinople was anything but "purely Christian." Constantine built a temple to Tyche, the guardian of the city, and to Rhea, an ancient "mother of the gods" whom the city of Byzantium had honored for centuries. A statue of Tyche accompanied the Christian emperor's own image in the Forum.[17] There is thus much evidence for a "syncretistic transition" from a pagan to a Christian empire, at least in the official symbolism.

On the other hand, there is some evidence that Constantine engaged in the active repression of paganism, at least later in his reign. Unfortunately most of our evidence comes from Eusebius, who clearly exaggerated the issue at some points. For example, his assertion that Constantine outlawed all sacrifice and image worship was wishful thinking. His claim that the emperor banned the worship of statues in Constantinople is contradicted by what we know about the syncretistic nature of the new capital as discussed above.[18] On the other hand, other references to the destruction of individual temples are probably correct; Constantine did indeed raze some pagan temples in order to replace them with Christian churches. These reports point to a selective destruction of pagan structures only when their existence interfered with Christian holy sites; there was no wholesale destruction of temples as Eusebius and other early Christian historians asserted.

In addition, legislation preserved from Constantine's reign took steps to outlaw certain forms of pagan religious practice. For example, the emperor banned soothsaying in private homes. The public practice, however, was still permitted; in fact, Constantine expressly ordered that soothsayers be consulted whenever lightning struck the imperial palace or other public buildings.[19] He proscribed magic deemed to be harmful to persons while allowing magic designed for healing or for agriculture. Such measures were politically safe. Few pagans would have objected to the outlawing of harmful magic, while even many pagans viewed private soothsaying as potentially subversive.

Constantine's steps against paganism were thus incremental, representing a shift from an apparent tolerance of pagan cult in the first decade of his reign to the beginnings of repression later on. An early letter of Constantine reveals the ambiguity that existed early in his reign, a combination of political toleration and personal intolerance.

> For it is one thing voluntarily to undertake the conflict for immortality, another to compel others to do so from fear of punishment.... We should indeed have earnestly recommended such removal [of pagan rites] to all men, were it not that the rebellious spirit of those wicked errors still continues obstinately fixed in the minds of some, so as to discourage the hope

of any general restoration of mankind to the ways of truth.[20]

On the surface, Constantine advocated tolerance for pagan cult, at least early in his reign. But it is clear that paganism was to give way, occasionally by force, when the interests of the two religions collided. Such collisions were to increase in both frequency and magnitude during the rule of his sons.

Of the sons of Constantine, the eldest, Constantine II, died in 340, only three years after his father; Constans' death in 350 left Constantius as sole ruler. All three sons carried out further steps in the repression of paganism, particularly Constantius. He finally outlawed pagan sacrifice upon pain of death; he ordered pagan temples closed in 346. Whether and how widely these edicts were enforced is subject to debate, but it is certain that Constantius was substantially more eager than his father to suppress pagan cult. During his reign there were popular Christian actions against pagans as well. In Cappadocian Caesarea, Christian mobs destroyed the temples of Zeus and Apollo; Julian later punished the same city for having the audacity to raze the temple of Tyche during his own reign. Julian's purge of Constantius' court upon his arrival in Constantinople would include those who had been "fattened on the robbery of temples"[21] during the reign of Constantius.

Paganism was far from disappearing outright, however. Legislation alone could not destroy paganism any more than it had been able to eliminate Christianity in previous centuries. Constantius' ban on sacrifices was only partially enforced, as public sacrifices continued to be offered on occasion.[22] In this mixed environment the repression begun under Constantine and accelerated under Constantius would form an important aspect of Julian's hostile stance towards the Christians.

> It was this that shook him to the core, as he saw their temples in ruins, their ritual banned, their altars overturned, their sacrifices suppressed, their priests sent packing and their property divided up between a crew of rascals.[23]

It was a situation that Julian believed he could reverse. Whether he could have stopped, or at least significantly slowed, the Christian tide had he lived longer is one of the most intriguing questions of the historiography of late antiquity.

We treat Julian in this study as an opponent of Christianity, and rightly so. He was, however, more than a critic; the emperor envisioned himself first and foremost as a restorer of religion. Whatever may be said about the sincerity of his uncle Constantine's faith in the Christian God, Julian's passionate belief in the gods is unquestioned. His anti-Christian stance must therefore be viewed in the context of his fervent paganism. After recounting briefly Julian's actions with respect to the church, we consider in this chapter two aspects of his reign that illustrate his attempt to restore paganism: his attempt to establish an organized form of pagan worship and his edict forbidding Christians to teach Greek literature.

In order to restore paganism to what he considered its proper place in society, Julian had to reverse the considerable advances the church had made in the previous fifty years. To this end he removed Christian clerics' exemption from public service; he reduced the lavish state subsidies the church had enjoyed, while pagan temples and priesthoods enjoyed imperial favor once again. His attitude toward the church establishment is revealed by his response to the lynching of the bishop of Alexandria by a pagan mob early in his reign; he took no action against the murderers, but merely chastised the citizenry in a letter for their conduct. Although no persecutor of Christians himself,[24] Julian appears not to have objected to anti-Christian violence when it occurred.

He understood, however, that the gains Christianity had made could not be undone overnight, and that merely favoring paganism would not accomplish his goal of religious restoration. The church was well-organized and growing steadily in popularity. In order to counter the strengths of the Christians, Julian attempted to reform pagan cult to establish what might be called a "pagan church" with Helios the sun-god as its central deity, using elements from Aurelian's cult of *Sol Invictus*. The new organization fielded a hierarchy of priests and a system of Neoplatonic doctrine, developed in part by Julian himself in the form of two treatises, *Hymn to King Helios* and *Hymn to the Mother of the Gods*. The new religious establishment also instituted a program of benevolence to the poor in order to counter the charitable activities of the Christians. He demanded high standards of conduct from pagan priests in opposition to what he considered the hypocritical behavior of Christian clerics. In short, the new state cult was to have many of the strengths of Christianity without its liabilities.

Julian's attempt to establish an alternative state religion never quite crystallized, partly because of his own untimely death. It may be legitimately asked whether the effort could have succeeded at all, given the strength of the church and the "artificial" nature of his reforms. His genius, however, was his recognition that a mere restoration of cult practice, funding, and architecture would have failed to win the hearts of ordinary people. At the very least Julian understood that nostalgia alone would not restore the religion he so highly valued, since he grasped many of the elements that attracted people to Christianity in the first place.[25]

One of the elements that had allowed Christianity to claim legitimacy over the course of the third and fourth centuries, especially among the upper classes, was its appropriation of Greek philosophy. We have discussed this process in earlier chapters; Justin had begun joining Christian theology to philosophy in the second century, a marriage consummated in the third century by Clement of Alexandria and especially by Origen. Tertullian's challenge, "What indeed has Athens to do with Jerusalem? What concord is there between the Academy and the Church?"[26] was answered by the church very much in the positive. The Christian appropriation of Platonism and Hellenistic literature continued apace through the fourth century to the point where an educated Christian was also a good Platonist. That Julian, still outwardly a Christian but a pagan at heart, could enjoy the company of the Christian theologian Basil as a classmate at the Athenian academy was a sign of how far the integration of the Christian and Hellenistic universes had proceeded.

Julian protested this integration as well as the resulting prestige that Christianity enjoyed. As far as he was concerned, the Christians' "theft" of the Hellenistic literary tradition was illegitimate; Christianity, by its rejection the gods, was opposed to everything the literature represented. Since pagan literature was inextricably linked to pagan religion, he considered the Christian use of such literature to be fundamentally dishonest.

Julian exposed this "dishonesty" on several levels. In the first place, the anthropomorphic biblical presentation of God had led Christians to the practice of allegory, which was to Julian an illegitimate method of "Hellenizing" the scriptures. Each biblical representation of the divine was "full of blasphemy against God, unless the phrase contains some occult and mysterious sense, which indeed I can suppose."[27] Of greater significance to Julian, however, was the ethical issue, an issue that was of central importance in his attempted restoration of paganism. Christianity was, in his view, an essentially impious and immoral religion, filled with hypocritical pretenders and political opportunists. The fact that Christians were such an immoral lot, he reasoned, must have been their purpose for appropriating Greek literature; even Christians understood that these writings were a better source of moral instruction than the Bible. "If the reading of your own scriptures is sufficient for you, why do you nibble at the learning of the Hellenes?"[28] For Julian, Hellenistic literature was a means to piety and great deeds, while the writings of the Jews and Christians were incapable of producing moral goodness. It was therefore the moral bankruptcy of the Christians, according to the critic, that led them to seek the "higher ground" of Greek literature.

In June 362, Julian took action designed to separate Christianity decisively from the Hellenistic literary tradition. He issued an edict specifying qualifications and procedures for the appointment of teachers; they "must excel first in character, then in eloquence." They were to be appointed by city councils with final approval by the emperor himself. Although the actual decree did not specifically bar Christians from teaching, Julian later clarified in a letter that this is exactly what he intended.[29] He believed that if he could divorce Christianity from the Hellenistic tradition, at least among the upper classes, he could turn back the clock on some of the progress the church had made over the previous century.

Predictably, Christians were outraged. A version of the Bible was immediately produced which rendered the Gospels into Socratic dialogue and much of the Hebrew Bible into Greek verse. Even the pagan historian Ammianus thought that Julian had gone too far: "But this one thing was inhumane, and ought to be buried in eternal silence, that he forbade teachers of rhetoric and literature to practice their profession, if they were followers of the Christian religion."[30] But whatever the judgment of pagan or Christian historians, the emperor's proclamation was absolutely consistent with his values. To Julian, Christianity and Hellenism were diametrically opposed on the cultural as well as the religious field of battle; the defense of

Hellenism as a way of life would form the central thesis of his critique of Christianity.

Julian's opposition to Christianity, legal as well as literary, was multi-faceted. As emperor his intention was to check and ultimately reverse the progress the church had made under the reign of Constantine and his sons. This concern is reflected not only in his polemic works but also in his decrees, both against the church and in favor of traditional paganism. Julian did not live long enough to take full advantage of the propaganda possibilities of coinage, on which he sported the philosopher's beard. He was not only a political figure, however; he also considered himself a philosopher, and it was in this role that he wrote *Against the Galileans* as well as other works. His extant literary output, unmatched by any other emperor, gives us a great deal of insight into the conservative wing of paganism during the decades in which that same paganism was being swept away.

However, the anti-Christian arguments of *Against the Galileans* cannot be examined in a literary vacuum. To a degree unparalleled for a Roman emperor, we have both his writings and a more than adequate record of his administration. It is the proper function of history in such cases to reconstruct the whole person and not merely his literature, which we have done in part by discussing his relevant legislation. We view Julian's arguments against the Christians in the context of what may rightly be characterized as his overriding concern: his passion for the greatness of Greek culture, the Hellenistic apology. Julian's defense of Hellenism formed the core of his attack on the Christians in both the literary and political arenas; in *Against the Galileans*, his original contributions to the argument against Christian exclusivism constitute much of the rhetorical ammunition. It is in this context that, like Porphyry, Julian employed a strategy of assimilation in order to exercise rhetorical control over his opponents.

Before proceeding to his polemic, it is necessary to establish a rhetorical context for Julian's arguments by examining his predecessors Celsus and Porphyry. This has been done in large measure in the preceding chapters. However, the state of scholarship on Julian's place within the history of anti-Christian polemic is inadequate, a fact that requires a somewhat more detailed comparison of the three critics than has been attempted before.

To do so requires that we establish a connection between the emperor and the anti-Christian polemic tradition, three centuries old by the time Julian ascended the throne. In some ways, as we have mentioned briefly, Julian's criticism of Christianity shared important features with those of Celsus and Porphyry. Christians, after all, had been under attack from various segments of the pagan world since the the church began; it is to be expected that after three centuries most of the major arguments would have been developed. Harnack's essentially correct if exaggerated remark that "Even today Porphyry remains unanswered"[31] testifies not so much to the genius of Porphyry's critique as to the permanence of the basic issues he raised, issues that reappear in Julian's treatise.

It is this endurance of the fundamentals of pagan anti-Christian polemic that scholars have tended to confuse with a lack of originality on Julian's part. Some have found no original thought at all in Julian's work, implying that he merely copied the arguments of his predecessors. Many are content to observe that there are a number of parallels between Julian and Celsus in particular and that Julian's arguments are much closer in tone and content to Celsus than to Porphyry. Typical is one scholar's characterization of *Against the Galileans* as "a disappointing book," "repetitive and woolly, unable to distinguish between the fundamental and the trivial" and lacking sustained argument.[32] Another writer's characterization of his work as being little more than "classical common sense" with its specifics traceable to Celsus[33] is incomplete and reflects a failure to examine Julian's work adequately. Julian was indeed the heir to three centuries of anti-Christian thought, and as such should be expected to use many of the same elements of the earlier polemic. But it is simply not true that "Julian's arguments against the Christian doctrine do not greatly differ from those used in the second century by Celsus, and by Porphyry in the third."[34]

That a comprehensive comparison of *Against the Galileans* with the works of Celsus and Porphyry has yet to be written should give pause when making such evaluations, as should the fact that Julian was the first to criticize Christianity after having himself been raised as a Christian. It is unknown to what extent Julian actually used the writings of Celsus and Porphyry, but it can be safely assumed that, given the impact Porphyry's *Against the Christians* was alleged to have made on Christians of the late third and early fourth centuries, Julian was probably familiar with its arguments. His use of Celsus' work is less certain, given its greater age; if, however, Julian was familiar with Christian apologetics, he would have had some exposure to Celsus' arguments as well. In any event, the issue of Julian's having actually used either of these works is largely irrelevant. The foundations of anti-Christian polemic, laid in large part by Celsus, continued to be built upon for the next two centuries. And while Julian's work is comparable to those of his predecessors on several points, his particular contribution to the anti-Christian project has not been adequately assessed.

The point of this excursus on scholarship regarding Julian is that understanding the differences between his anti-Christian arguments and those of Celsus and Porphyry is crucial to grasping Julian's particular polemic strategy. This strategy may be observed in part by comparing specific lines of reasoning in *Against the Galileans* with those same arguments as his predecessors employed them. Julian was in many ways an original thinker when it came to criticizing his Christian opponents; and while this chapter has placed him in his historical context, our task in the next chapter will be to locate him within a particular literary context—as the culmination of the pagan anti-Christian rhetorical tradition.

6

Julian and the Bounded God

To do justice to Julian's polemic work against the Christians would take much more discussion than can be accomplished here. Instead, this chapter locates him within the established anti-Christian rhetorical tradition by examining three of his specific arguments, all of which had already been articulated in earlier form by his predecessors Celsus and Porphyry. The first argument concerns the general use of Judaism as a "weapon" in pagan anti-Christian polemic. Julian's criticism of the Jewish origins of Christianity signals an important change of attitude towards Judaism, especially when compared with that of Celsus. As we will see, Julian's criticism of Judaism was carefully nuanced in such a way as to target specifically the Jewish literary tradition in order to defend the Hellenistic, a nuance that will also represent a central element in his rhetoric of assimilation.

The second argument we consider refers back to the pagan theology, articulated by Celsus, of divine overseers for each nation. Julian coalesced the doctrine into a powerful exposure of the contradiction within Christianity between the universal and the particular, between God's status as the guardian of a particular people and that of supreme deity. The third argument, known through Justin and used explicitly by Porphyry, is that Christ's late coming consigned the vast majority of the human race to eternal condemnation. Julian's specific usage of, and contributions to, these arguments enabled him to establish a polemic boundary between Christianity and Hellenistic culture, a boundary crucial to his defense of the latter.

The importance of these three points is that, taken together, they reveal as the organizing principle of Julian's polemic his *apologia* for the cultural and religious aspects of Hellenism. Like Celsus, he established rhetorical boundaries between Christianity and Hellenism. On the other hand, like Porphyry, he accepted portions of Christian belief in order to draw boundaries within Christianity itself. By using the works of Celsus and Porphyry as bases for comparison, we can examine Julian's specific contributions to what were otherwise well-worn lines of anti-Christian argument.

The pagan objection that Christians were in reality apostates from Judaism was prominent in Celsus' *True Doctrine*. The fact that Christians—both those who were Jews originally and those who had converted from paganism—had left the religion of their ancestors was an important weapon in Celsus' polemic and was evidence that Christians were an impious lot. That this particular accusation served as standard anti-Christian fare is evident by its appearance in all three of the critics examined in this study. Julian made much use of it, while Porphyry had complained that Christians rejected the sacrifices and temple worship of the Jewish law, even though their own scriptures required it.

At the same time, it must be remembered that pagan polemicists used Judaism as a "two-edged sword" against the Christians. In the first place, whatever the critics disapproved of in Judaism or in the Hebrew Bible they also charged against the Christians. On the other hand, they condemned Christians for departing from whatever was laudable in Judaism, such as its antiquity or its sacrificial system. Thus when pagans used Judaism to criticize Christianity the sword could cut in either direction, either in the manner of "guilt by association" with elements of Judaism that the critic found objectionable, or in the form of contrasting the practices of the renegade Christians with the praiseworthy Jewish practices they left behind. The persistence of these arguments makes it natural that they should appear in Julian's polemic. And they do; in *Against the Galileans* the sword indeed swings in both directions.

However, the issue becomes more complex when we compare Julian's rhetoric with that of the earlier polemicists since we possess additional material from which to evaluate his attitude toward Jews and Judaism. We have no such information for Celsus, as he is known only through Origen's quotations of the *True Doctrine*; although we have more literary sources for Porphyry, it is still difficult to characterize clearly his stance toward the Jews. Our more comprehensive knowledge of Julian allows us to evaluate his actions as well as his words; by studying his overall view of Judaism we are able to evaluate his use of Judaism in his anti-Christian polemic.

It would be helpful at this point to place our study of Julian and the Jews in the context of earlier scholarship on this issue. Julian has been variously called a sincere Jewish sympathizer and an opportunist with no love at all for the Jews. A century ago, Michael Adler remarked that the history of of Judaism under more rulers like Julian "would have been considerably brighter, illumined by the warm glow of a generous tolerance and intelligent sympathy."[1] Most other commentators have rightly assigned more *Realpolitik* to Julian's motives; Yohanan Lewy, for example, noted that his hatred of Christians, more than his love for Jews, motivated his project (discussed below) of rebuilding the temple in Jerusalem.[2] John G. Gager's balanced treatment of Julian's own mixed statements regarding the Jews concludes that, like other Neoplatonists, the emperor was "genuinely attracted to certain aspects" of Judaism.[3]

Because of the sometimes equivocal nature of the these statements of Julian, we would do well to heed David Rokeah's warning regarding the contextualization of Jewish-Christian-pagan polemic.

> Since Judaism served the pagans and Christians alike as a weapon for the purpose of their ideological conflict, we witness the modification of their attitudes towards Judaism and Jewish traditions in keeping with the interests of the parties concerned, even when this involved the relaxation of formerly firm positions, or the offering of mutually contradictory explications.[4]

Even this statement requires qualification, however. While Rokeah's observation keeps us from reading too dogmatically those statements regarding the Jews that appear in a polemic context, it is also possible to oversimplify "the interests of the parties concerned." Since pagan polemicists did not share identical interests, Julian's use of Judaism was much different from that of Celsus and even of Porphyry. The manner in which they used Judaism differed greatly according to the historical and political contexts of the critics as well as the particular rhetorical strategies they chose to employ.

Thus the importance, in the case of Julian, of considering his specific actions toward the Jews in addition to his polemic. These actions indicate that he generally favored them, in policy if not always in genuine respect. For example, he abolished special taxes that earlier emperors had levied against the Jews. His most dramatic move, though, was to authorize the rebuilding of the Jewish temple. Having learned during a meeting with Jewish leaders in Antioch that they were permitted to perform animal sacrifice only at the temple at Jerusalem, destroyed during the first Jewish revolt in 70 CE, he gave permission and funding for the Jews to begin rebuilding the temple on its former site. The motivations for Julian's decision are still being debated, just as they were in the fourth and fifth centuries.[5] While his enthusiasm for blood sacrifice was certainly one reason, other Christian writers of the period pointed to a desire on the part of Julian to disprove the Christian teaching about the eternal desolation of the temple. Although most treatments of the problem have emphasized his religious motivations, one biographer has pointed out possible political motivations for the project: Julian realized that the Jews had supported the rival Persians in the past and that he should court this substantial Eastern minority.[6] His elimination of the tax that the Jews had paid to the Jewish patriarchy was perhaps intended as a prelude to an eventual transfer of power within Judaism from the patriarchate to what would become a new temple establishment. In any event, construction was begun, but an earthquake and fire hindered the work, and the project was eventually abandoned.

His actions, especially the attempt to rebuild the temple, have generated disagreement regarding Julian's attitude toward the Jews. Did he merely exploit them for his anti-Christian purposes or did he genuinely favor them? As we have indicated, it is difficult to answer such a question based on his writings alone; his references to Judaism do not serve as trustworthy indicators when polemic ends are in view. The same caution applies in interpreting his actions with regard to the Jews, embroiled as he was in a hostile relationship with the church. In the end, it is probably unwise to separate too rigorously the options of genuine regard and political exploitation. Julian was, after all, raised as a Christian and therefore received Christian teaching about the Jews, little of it positive. As an adult, the idealistic pagan and enemy of Christianity may have had some genuine admiration for Jewish law. The most likely description of his view of Judaism is that, while Judaism served as a customary and effective stick with which to beat the Christians, there were at the same time elements of Judaism that resonated positively with him, such as its antiquity and the fact that its scriptures required blood sacrifice. Although there is no doubt that he viewed Judaism as inferior to paganism, he nonetheless had some kind of actual regard for the Jews—especially, of course, when they served his anti-Christian policies and polemic.

With this somewhat ambivalent characterization in hand we are now in a position to examine the role the Jews played in his anti-Christian polemic, particularly as this role related to the Hellenistic apology. Julian, like his predecessors, accused the Christians of being duplicitous in their claim to have their origins in Judaism while at the same time rejecting everything important about the Jewish religion such as Sabbath observance, circumcision, and *kashrut*. Similar to the way in which Celsus accused the Christians of being Jewish apostates, Julian noted their abandonment of both Judaism and Hellenism, asking why they were

> neither Hellenes nor Jews, but belong to the sect of the Galileans, why they preferred the belief of the Jews to ours; and what, further, can be the reason why they do not even adhere to the Jewish beliefs but have abandoned them also and followed a way of their own. For they have not accepted a single admirable or important doctrine of those that are held either by us Hellenes or by the Hebrews who derived them from Moses. . .[7]

Like both Celsus and Porphyry before him, Julian criticized the Christians for leaving their Jewish roots. There is an important difference, however, between Julian's treatment of this issue and that of his predecessors, especially Celsus. For Celsus, the Christians' guilt in leaving Judaism lay solely in the fact that they had abandoned an ancestral religion; there was nothing inherently favorable about Judaism that the Christians could be blamed for leaving behind. Jewish monotheism and exclusivism were detestable to Celsus; his characterization of Moses and the Exodus as a flight of renegade Egyptians, while reinforcing the theme of apostasy, served to accentuate his criticism of the Jews as a barbarian race. According to Celsus, the only redeeming quality that Judaism possessed was its antiquity.

Julian, on the other hand, whatever his motivations might have been regarding the temple project, had a more favorable outlook on the Jews than had Celsus. To be sure, he was critical of some aspects of Judaism. For example, a major portion of the extant fragments of *Against the Galileans* is devoted to criticizing the Jewish doctrine of creation, comparing it unfavorably to the Platonic version in the *Timaeus*. But as we will see, this was no random selection of Jewish targets to attack, as Celsus' polemic largely was. For the most part, Julian criticized the Christians for abandoning their Jewish ancestry, separating his opponents from a generally favorable Judaism.

Even while driving a wedge between Christians and their Jewish origins, Julian did allow one explicit connection between the two religions. Importantly, the only aspect of Judaism which Julian explicitly credited Christianity with having retained was its theological exclusivism. Even on this point, however, Julian asserted that Judaism in its original state had not been so exclusive. According to Julian, even exclusivism was a later addition to Judaism, implying that an original "pure Judaism" allowed for the existence of the gods. His translation of Exodus 22:28, "Thou shalt not revile the gods," as well as the Genesis 6 account of the "sons of God" provided biblical evidence for both their existence and their exalted nature. Important also was Julian's claim that, with the exception of exclusivism, there was actually little difference between a pagan and a Jew, since

> the Jews agree with the Gentiles, except that they believe in only one God. That is indeed peculiar to them and strange to us; since all the rest we have in a manner in common with them—temples, sanctuaries, altars, purifications, and certain precepts. For as to these we differ from one another either not at all or in trivial matters.[8]

Julian, then, was no indiscriminate critic of Judaism, striking out at the Jews with hopes of landing some blows on the Christians in the process. Instead, he sought to demonstrate at the expense of Christianity the relative reasonableness of the religion they left behind. He praised the Jews for their dietary laws and sacrifice, although he clearly believed that Judaism was inferior to paganism. He accused Christians of misusing Jewish prophecy and failing to keep many aspects of Jewish law. The crime of the Christians, then, was to abandon the praiseworthy practices of both Jews and Hellenes in order to embrace the worship of "the corpse" and "many wretched men,"[9] namely Jesus and the saints. His use of Judaism as a weapon of anti-Christian polemic differed greatly from that of Celsus in that, for the most part, the emperor used a strategy of Christian contrast with Judaism instead of a strategy of association.

When Julian did explicitly use the latter approach, it was quite specific and limited to the Christian appropriation of a "non-authentic" Jewish exclusivism. In addition to this explicit use, however, there is an important way in which Julian formed an implicit link between Christianity and Judaism. Besides his attack on Jewish and Christian exclusivism, he devoted a large portion of *Against the Galileans*[10] to a critique of the Genesis account of creation, a criticism that is at least an implicit attack on Judaism. Although asserting at one point that theological exclusivism was the only aspect of Judaism that Christianity retained, the creation account provided Julian with an additional means of associating Christianity with Judaism.

However, this attack on the Jewish doctrine of creation is quite circumspect; it does not take the form of conventional anti-Jewish polemic. Specifically, Julian criticized the Jewish mythology without criticizing the Jews. Why is this the case? Why did he not merely attack the Jewish doctrine of creation, label it as philosophically unsophisticated and logically incoherent, and then attribute those faults to the beliefs of Jews and Christians alike? After all, such an approach would have been standard procedure for Celsus. In the first place, Julian's more guarded approach was consistent with his generally favorable regard of Judaism. In the process of criticizing an important aspect of Jewish belief, Julian refused to turn the critique into a round of anti-Jewish polemic, even as the opportunity presented itself. More important still, the purpose of *Against the Galileans* required a much more sophisticated tactic than that of "guilt by association." In his polemic work Julian was attempting to defend Hellenism, a purpose that was at least as important to him as his critique of Christianity.

How did his criticism of the creation account serve this purpose? Julian's point-by-point comparison of the biblical creation story with Plato's account of creation in the *Timaeus* was intended to demonstrate above all that the Hellenistic account provided satisfactory answers to a number of important theological questions, while the Genesis account did not. For example, according to Julian, since Genesis does not explain the origin of matter, it is evident that God merely used pre-existing material for the process of creation, leaving unexplained the origin of the matter with which God worked. In addition the Bible, although admitting in several passages that the gods do in fact exist, does not give an account of their origin.

Therefore, according to Julian, the scriptures are incomplete and inconsistent, omitting as they do several important aspects of the origin of the universe. The Platonic account in the *Timaeus*, on the other hand, explains the origin of both the material universe and the gods.

Julian's immediate objective in making these comparisons is clear. The creation account in the *Timaeus*, characterized by clarity, consistency and a full explanation of reality, is superior to the biblical account, which is ambiguous, self-contradictory and lacking information. But there was a larger object in view. Julian was doing more than comparing two accounts of creation, although that was the immediate problem, "in order that we may compare Plato's account of that generation [of the universe] with that of Moses." His more important goal was the comparison of two composers of literature, Moses and Plato.

> For in this way it will appear who was the nobler and who was more worthy of intercourse with God, Plato who paid homage to images, or he of whom the Scripture says that God spake with him mouth to mouth.[11]

Thus Julian's comparison of the rival accounts of creation was not simply an argument for the existence of the gods, nor was it even primarily a philosophical argument for the Hellenistic over the Mosaic accounts of creation. It was more than anything an argument for the superiority of Greek literature over its Hebrew counterpart, of Plato over Moses, the so-called "worshiper of idols" over the one with whom God talked "mouth to mouth"—the latter expression probably a dig at Jewish and Christian anthropomorphism. For Julian, the comparison was every bit as much a literary contest as it was a philosophical and theological one.

Julian was therefore accomplishing more with this argument than simply an attack on a Jewish creation myth that he found objectionable. He was above all engaged in the defense of the cultural construct of Hellenism. This culture consisted of several specific elements. It included Greek literature, Greek philosophy as enshrined in the writings of Plato and his interpreters, polytheistic religion (it was no accident that Julian referred to Plato as "the idolater," since the emperor considered polytheism an integral part of Platonism), and the accomplishments of Roman government. This argument regarding the doctrine of creation is in many ways representative of Julian's apologetic approach throughout *Against the Galileans*. Although the attack on the Genesis account of creation was indirectly an argument against Christian theology, it is more properly to be interpreted as an apologetic for Greek literature and the associated culture that Christianity threatened.

Julian's discussion carries another important implication, namely that he was employing a new strategy on an old polemic battlefield. Previously, Celsus had held up Jewish myth as an object of ridicule, as so barbaric and incredible that Jews and Christians alike had to make illegitimate use of allegory in order to make them intelligible. Celsus' purpose had been to demonstrate that Christians, because of their Jewish origins, were as worthy of ridicule and rejection as the Jews. Julian's treatment of Jewish creation myth, however, had a more specific purpose than merely to attack Christianity at the expense of Judaism. He selected the Genesis creation account and other targets with care and precision in order to accomplish specific rhetorical objectives. Since Julian's positive attitude toward Judaism prevented him from broadly associating Jews and Christians as a single group of undesirables, Judaism served a polemic purpose substantially different from that of Celsus, a difference missed by virtually all interpreters of the emperor Julian. And while the Hellenistic apology was the primary focus of Julian's use of Judaism, he deployed in the process a rhetorical strategy of assimilation—a deployment we will examine more closely in the following section.

Celsus in the *True Doctrine* had argued that, instead of choosing which deities were worthy of worship, everyone should revere the gods of their ancestors. His objection was essentially ethical in nature. Abandoning one's traditional gods was to Celsus the greatest form of impiety, even if that traditional religion was Judaism. But he also offered a theological justification for this ethical imperative, namely that each nation was possessed of certain divine "overseers" appointed by the supreme deity, each one responsible for the well-being and governance of its particular nation and ethnic group. In fact the entire earth, Celsus maintained, had been divided from the beginning among the various deities. Therefore all Christians, whether they had been converted from Judaism or paganism, were guilty of transgressing the boundaries of their ancestral religions, established by the gods of the various peoples of the empire. According to Celsus, then, the impiety of the Christians consisted primarily of abandoning the deities that had been originally assigned for their governance.

But although there was a theological dimension to Celsus' argument, the thrust of his appeal was ultimately ethical. It was not until Julian that the objection shifted from a violation of Græco-Roman piety to the status of a fundamental contradiction within Christian theology. This contradiction, according to Julian, was that the Christian God held two "offices" at the same time: that of supreme God and that of a national deity.

This tension had formed a deep and lasting current within Christian theology from the very beginning of the church. The God of the Christians was in fact the deity of a particular people, namely the Jews. The larger church never abandoned this aspect of its origin. The Christians, however, advanced at the same time the claim that this deity was the supreme God, the creator of the universe and of all the nations of the world. Since Justin Martyr they had been identifying their God with the supreme Platonic principle as well. The Christians were thus putting forth two seemingly irreconcilable claims: that their God was on the one hand universal, but on the other hand national and local, a theological claim they shared with the Jews.[12]

There was no escaping the tension for the simple reason that Christianity could not make a complete break with its Jewish heritage. Marcion and the movement he founded in the middle of the second century had made such an attempt. His condemnation by the larger church demonstrated that Christianity would not separate itself completely from its Jewish roots. One consequence of this decision, however, was that the church's Jewish origin became a standard component of the pagan criticism of Christianity. Part of this criticism lay in the fact that Christians, although claiming to be the spiritual heirs of Judaism, by and large did not obey certain important requirements of the Jewish law; they did not circumcise, observe the Sabbath or keep kosher. To be sure, there were still Christians, particularly in the eastern part of the empire, whom John Chrysostom would chastise at the end of the fourth century for observing Jewish practices and holidays.

The festivals of the wretched and miserable Jews which follow one after another in succession—Trumpets, Booths, the Fasts—are about to take place. And many who belong to us and say that they believe in our teaching, attend their festivals, and even share in their celebrations and join in their fasts. It is this evil practice I now wish to drive from the church.[13]

In general, however, issues of religious practice tended to separate rather than unite Jews and Christians. The church's closest link to Judaism was the Hebrew Bible, and it was these scriptures that pagan critics seized upon to attack the Christian theology of God. Although portraying God as the universal creator, the Jewish scriptures that the Christians had adopted clearly presented this same God as a tribal deity. Furthermore, to most pagans this deity seemed unreasonably exclusive, ordering the destruction of other temples and their gods and forbidding his followers to accommodate themselves to the customs of other peoples. Thus in the view of many pagans the God of the Jews and the Christians was not only the deity of a minority people but a xenophobe to boot. How, they asked, could such traits be attributed to the God who ostensibly created all the peoples of the world?

This tension was not lost on Julian. Like Celsus earlier, he objected that the anthropomorphic, jealous God of the Jews and Christians could not be identified with the Platonic One that the Christians claimed was theirs. Human traits such as anger and petty jealousy were inadmissible in speaking about such a God. Celsus had focused mainly upon divine jealousy as an ethical problem; it seemed from his perspective to be the cause of the Christians' impious exclusivism. Julian's primary focus, on the other hand, was geographical and ethnic.

> Now I will only point out that Moses himself and the prophets who came after him and Jesus the Nazarene, yes and Paul also, who surpassed all the magicians and charlatans of every place and every time, assert that he is the God of Israel alone and of Judaea, and that the Jews are his chosen people.[14]

According to Julian, the Jewish and Christian scriptures themselves disqualified God from the status of universal deity. Both God's choosing of Israel in the Hebrew Bible and the incarnation of that same God in the New Testament were purely local phenomena, incompatible with the greatness and universality of the supreme divinity postulated by the Greeks and Romans. It was inconceivable to Julian that a truly cosmic deity could be confined to a specific locality and people, a fact that led Julian to call the Christians "Galileans."[15]

In the extant anti-Christian polemic, this contradiction between the universal and the particular is unique to Julian. However, he did not stop with merely observing the existence of the difficulty in Christian theology, a difficulty whose tension had been at least an instinctive component of church life since the time of Marcion. Julian's more important contribution was that he integrated the particular criticism into a larger element of pagan belief, namely the theology of the national overseers discussed earlier; and further, that he demonstrated this integration from the Hebrew Bible itself.

Julian argued that the Bible's own characterization of God as a local (and hence insignificant) deity—"the God of Israel alone," as he put it—made this God ineligible for consideration as the supreme deity. For instance, in Julian's critique of the story of the tower of Babel (Genesis 11:1–9) he observed that the God of the Bible superintended the division of languages among humanity. However, Julian continued, are there not much greater differences among the nations than merely that of language? Important cultural and even physical differences divide the human race by their respective nationalities. Especially significant and noteworthy are variations in "national personality"; the Germans, Julian argued, are naturally warlike while the Romans are "inclined to political life and humane."[16] Since differences in language constitute an insignificant element in the division of the nations, the deity who confounded the languages at Babel actually performed a very minor act indeed.

> If the immediate creator of the universe be he who is proclaimed by Moses, then we hold nobler beliefs concerning him, inasmuch as we consider him to be the master of all things in general. . ."[17]

According to Julian, the Jews and Christians worshiped a far more insignificant god than either the supreme deity of Platonism or the major deities of the Græco-Roman pantheon. The God of the Christians was nothing more than a local overseer.

For this reason, Julian considered complete nonsense the Christian idea that the God of the Jews should also be the God of the gentiles. Paul practiced such double talk when he exclaimed, "Is God the God of Jews only? Is he not the God of Gentiles too? Yes, of Gentiles too. . ." (Romans 3:29). Julian considered that this deity, while worthy of some degree of honor, was not worthy of elevation to such exalted status.

> But if Moses first pays honour to a sectional god, and then makes the lordship of the whole universe contrast with his power, then it is better to believe as we do, and to recognise the God of the All, though not without apprehending also the God of Moses; this is better, I say, than to honour one who has been assigned the lordship over a very small portion, instead of the creator of all things.[18]

Thus the god of the Christians, according to Julian, was not only a mere local god but a petty usurper as well. Originally given lordship over an insignificant area of the world and over a particular people, this deity had wrongfully been assigned a higher office. Although worthy of some limited amount of honor, his worshipers had granted to him that which was not rightly his, namely the status of creator of the universe and supreme being.

We are now in a position to summarize Julian's treatment of the Christian doctrine of God. In *Against the Galileans* he laid bare what he considered the fundamental contradiction in Jewish and Christian theology, that the deity of these two religions was at the same time universal and particular. Although hinted at by Celsus, it was Julian who explicitly pointed out the issue with all its implications. As the Jewish and Christian scriptures themselves testify, God chose the nation of the Jews to be his very own; his laws and benefits were for the Jews alone. Even the New Testament doctrine of the incarnation revealed a God limited in time and space. How could it be possible for the same deity to claim to be the sovereign of all peoples and the creator of the world?

Not satisfied simply to point out the theological tension, Julian took sides in the issue, firmly declaring the God of the Jews and Christians to be nothing more than a regional god. To Julian, this was as true for Judaism as it was for Christianity; "[The Jews'] cardinal error is that they have raised to the status of supreme and only God a divinity who was merely of local and national importance."[19]

Julian's central point in employing the theology of national overseers was that the Jewish and Christian God was exactly that: a
national deity and nothing more. In *Against the Galileans*, he attempted to put the divine usurper back in his place.

However, there was more to Julian's argument than a desire to
demote Israel's God. The theology of the national overseers and its
implications for God provided a vehicle for Julian's larger project,
which was to draw the distinction between Christian and Hellene.
This distinction was being blurred by the Christian appropriation
of Hellenistic literature, an appropriation that Julian viewed as illegitimate and ultimately harmful to Græco-Roman culture. The
Christian violation of "divine boundaries" represented by the promotion of the Jewish God to supreme status was more than a
theological issue for Julian. More important, it was a threat to the
Hellenism he was attempting to restore. In other words, the worship of a supreme deity who was fundamentally opposed to
Hellenistic culture in every way could have nothing but devastat-
ing consequences for that same culture. Thus the metaphor of
"usurpation" applies to the cultural as well as theological realm, the
illegitimate Christian appropriation of Hellenistic literature acting
as a parallel problem to the illegitimate elevation of a local deity to
supreme status. In this same vein it would not be pressing the image too far to remember that Julian viewed himself as the divinely
appointed restorer of religion, using his imperial power to put down
a cultural as well as theological rebellion.

But even if Julian's concern was to put the Jewish and Christian
deity in his place, such a place was nonetheless a legitimate one in
the emperor's religious world view. Contrary to Celsus' anti-Jewish strategy, Julian's theology of defining the God of the Christians
as an ethnic and local deity served the purpose of further legitimizing Judaism. Celsus had previously employed the tactic of
dismissing the Jews altogether in his attempt to marginalize the
Christians; he had made no attempt to offer theological significance
to the Jewish God. Julian, on the other hand, retained a place for the
God of the Bible in the form of an ethnic religion. It was a limited
place to be sure, but no more limited than that of other local or ethnic deities. Furthermore, and perhaps more important, he managed
to integrate theologically the God of Judaism into the broader universe of Græco-Roman religion. For example, Julian's interpretation

of the Tower of Babel story allowed the Jewish God a mythical place in universal human history, namely the division of humanity into different language groups. A minor role, of course, but the critic was nevertheless attempting to establish a place for Judaism in the larger household of universal paganism. With this perspective, we may interpret Julian's claim that Judaism was not originally an exclusive religion as a clearly marked entrance through which the Jews could enter. It was an attempt at theological assimilation, punctuated in the concrete by his decree authorizing the rebuilding of the temple in Jerusalem. At the same time, such a strategy of assimilation allows a satisfying integration of both his actions and his writings with regard to his attitude toward Judaism. His positive regard for the Jews carried with it a theological price tag: a non-exclusive Judaism, its deity absorbed into the pagan pantheon.

This examination of Julian's rhetorical strategy also allows us to propose a new theory as to his motivations for undertaking the project of rebuilding the temple. We may view his authorization for the rebuilding as a political manifestation of his overall anti-Christian strategy, especially if we postulate a measure of consistency between his anti-Christian rhetoric and his policies; after all, consistency is usually a characteristic of idealists such as Julian. While the rebuilding has historically been viewed as an attempt to prove false the Christian teaching regarding the eternal desolation of the temple, a much more ambitious motive is suggested here. It must be remembered that the God who was to be worshiped at the restored temple was not only the God of the Jews, but the God of the Christians as well, since they were in fact one and the same deity. For Julian, the temple project would have done much more than merely contradict an obscure Christian prophecy. It would also have accomplished more than simply allow the Jews to offer blood sacrifices in an authorized location. Of course, both of these issues were probably concerns of the emperor. However, by directing the rebuilding of the temple in Jerusalem, Julian was trying to restore the Christian God to his original (and far less significant) place. "Restricting" the Christians' deity to a particular location would have been a powerful tool by which to undermine their claims to universality and exclusivism. Once the temple was built and in operation, how would the Christians be able to claim that their God, even now receiving animal sacrifices in an insignificant Judean town, was the universal supreme deity? At the same time, it is difficult to dismiss the visual effect of a restored Jewish temple only a few hundred yards from the venerated Church of the Holy Sepulchre in Jerusalem.

In addition, having sacrifices offered there for the benefit of a pagan state would have ultimately served the purpose of "domesticating" the God of the Christians for pagan use. Although the sacrifices would have been performed by a restored Jewish priesthood, Julian's motives were clear in this regard: blood sacrifices were to be offered, wherever possible, to powerful deities—including the God of the Jews and Christians—in the interests of the Roman Empire. What greater victory could Julian have achieved over the Christians than by making their religion nothing more than another local cult in the service of a pagan state? Whether or not such an arrangement would have had any lasting consequences for the church or its growth, the symbolic effect would have been just what the emperor ordered.

This suggestion of Julian's motive for the temple project emerges from the discussion regarding his attitude toward the Jews, a discussion with two implications for our study. In the first place, it highlights and clarifies the polemicist's use of the Jews as a weapon against the Christians. As stated previously, the standard approach to the pagan use of Judaism in anti-Christian polemic has been either a rhetoric of Christian association with an objectionable Judaism or one of contrast with the religion they abandoned. Julian's approach, when viewed in both its literary and political contexts, is significantly more complex and nuanced than either of these options. It is the subtlety of Julian's consciously crafted strategy with respect to the Jews, combined with the failure of most interpreters to integrate this strategy into the emperor's larger project of the Hellenistic apology, that has led students of Julian to disagree regarding his motivations.

Second, our discussion of Julian and the Jews helps us to locate the emperor in the development of anti-Christian polemic over the nearly two centuries covered by this study. Julian's favor toward Judaism constituted a central element of his rhetorical strategy of assimilation. His acceptance of Judaism, the God of the Jews and Christians, and several aspects of the biblical ceremonial law provide evidence of a strategy designed to marginalize Christianity by incorporating elements favorable to Julian. Naturally, this acceptance was conditioned on a reconstruction of Judaism that made it more friendly to paganism. We may compare this phenomenon in Julian's polemic with Porphyry's favorable regard for Jesus as an immortal, which was a tactic designed to exercise control over the person of Jesus by "domesticating" him for pagan use. Julian's incorporation of the Jews and Judaism within the boundaries of pagan discourse followed a similar strategy of assimilating the Jewish elements of Christian theology in order to exercise control over them. Because of the Christians' dominant political position, the elimination of Christianity was no longer an option, even in a rhetorical sense; the target of Julian's polemic and politics was an enemy whose position was to be carefully manipulated, not destroyed. At least, not yet.

This manipulation included the deployment of traditional anti-Christian arguments by new and more effective means. We have examined two of these so far, namely the Christian association with Judaism and the theology of the divine overseers, with their implications for Julian's ideological agenda. The third involves the objection to Christianity's recent origin. By the time Julian acquired the purple, Christianity had been on the scene for more than three centuries. Relative to most of the other religions of the Mediterranean basin, however, it was still as much a newcomer as it had been when Celsus accused it of being an "innovative" sect. That Christians were still having to defend themselves from this charge at the turn of the fourth century is evident from the apologetic of Eusebius, who found it necessary to assert that Christianity was in fact the most ancient of all religions. Since even the patriarchs of the Hebrew Bible, he maintained, engaged in the pure worship of the one God, "they therefore shared the name of Christ with us."[20]

The recent origin of Christianity provided more than an opportunity for pagans to charge Christians with religious innovation, important as that accusation was with respect to the value system of antiquity. As discussed earlier, the church's recent origin coupled with its claim to exclusivity posed a special problem: what was the fate of those who lived before the coming of Christ? If Jesus is the only way to God, why was this way not revealed long before? The question was particularly aimed at Christian exclusivism, since a religion that did not make the exclusive claim would not have been open to this kind of critique. As noted previously, the objection had been raised as early as the time of Justin Martyr and was articulated by Porphyry. The objection to the logical problem of an exclusive revelation limited to recent time was powerful and persistent.

However, it is not until Julian that we find this specific argument integrated with the tension between Christian (and Jewish) theological universalism and ethnic particularism, a target of contradiction that Julian believed demonstrable from both testaments of the Bible. According to Julian, the fact that the Christian revelation was localized in geography and ethnicity was at least as problematic as the fact that Christ had come only recently in time.

> And finally God sent unto [the Jews] Jesus also, but unto us no prophet, no oil of anointing, no teacher, no herald to announce his love for man which should one day, though late, reach even unto us also. Nay he even looked on for myriads, or if you prefer, for thousands of years, while men in extreme ignorance served idols, as you call them, from where the sun rises to where he sets, yes and from North to South, save only that little tribe which less than two thousand years before had settled in one part of Palestine. For if he is the God of all of us alike, and the creator of all, why did he neglect us?[21]

On the surface, this argument is no more than a repetition of the argument of Porphyry and others before him. The God of the entire world allowed that same world to live in error before the coming of Christ, an argument that invalidated the Christian claim to exclusivity. Importantly, however, Julian added the issue of the limitation of God's revelation to Palestine and the Jews. Julian exposed the tension not only between Christian exclusivism and the temporal nature of the revelation, but also between Christian universalism and the localization of God's revelation to Israel and the Jews alone. He thus juxtaposed the classic objection to Christianity's recent advent with the contradiction he articulated between the universal and particular in Judaism and Christianity.

Unlike Porphyry, however, Julian was not content merely to expose the contradiction and allow the resulting tension to carry the weight of the argument. Julian provided an answer, one that is not surprising given what we have discovered thus far, namely that the God of the Jews and Christians was in fact merely a local deity:

Wherefore it is natural to think that the God of the Hebrews was not the begetter of the whole universe with lordship over the whole, but rather, as I said before, that he is confined within limits, and that since his empire has bounds we must conceive of him as only one of the crowd of other gods.[22]

According to Julian, then, the recent arrival of the Christian faith, coupled with the fact that this arrival was limited to Palestine and the Jews, must force the thinking person to accept that the God of the Christians was not the supreme creator of the universe. By reformulating the earlier argument of Porphyry into a choice between accepting the Christian God as the "begetter of the whole universe" and accepting him as nothing more than the God of the Jews, Julian rejected Christian universalism by choosing the latter.

Importantly, Julian affirmed at the same time the "bounds" of God's empire, a meager empire at that, consisting only of the "little tribe" of the Jews. Using the argument against the late arrival of Christ, Julian painted a picture of a God limited in time in much the same way that, as we observed in the previous section, he limited God with regard to geography and ethnicity. According to Julian, a deity who reveals himself only at particular times to a particular nationality cannot be the supreme God. By placing rhetorical controls—temporal, geographic, and ethnic—on the boundaries of Christian theology, Julian separated the Christian and Jewish God from the supreme God of the universe, a division that was a crucial component of the Hellenistic apology.

We may now observe how Julian exploited this division. Basing many of his arguments upon those that Celsus and Porphyry had used earlier, Julian expanded and altered them in order to establish a rhetorical boundary between Christianity and Hellenism. Because of Julian's passion for Hellenistic culture, it is not surprising that a large section of *Against the Galileans* contrasts the achievements of that culture with those of the Jews. The Hellenistic world, according to Julian, perfected science and philosophy from their Egyptian and Babylonian origins; the Greeks themselves developed law, while the Romans perfected government. For the purpose of healing the bodies and souls of people, the gods gave Asclepius to humanity as "the greatest of the gifts of Helios and Zeus,"[23] a reminder that pagan religion could not be separated from the greatness of Hellenistic culture. Julian contrasted all these achievements and gifts of the gods with the achievements of the Jews: "But what great gift of this sort do the Hebrews boast of as bestowed on them by God, the Hebrews who have persuaded you [Christians] to desert to them?"[24]

Julian proceded to argue that the Jews had never had a great empire or culture. They had, he noted, very rarely lived as a free nation over the previous two thousand years. Julian argued that the Jews had never matched the Greeks and Romans in the administration of cities, their courts of law, or in their learning; that the wisdom of Solomon was nothing to boast about, especially since the king himself had been a fool; that the Jews produced no Hippocrates as a physician, no Alexander as a general. In every possible category by which one can measure the greatness of a civilization, according to Julian, the Jewish culture was inferior to the Hellenistic.

Again, however, Julian's criticism of Judaism served a larger purpose in the polemic; grasping his rhetorical use of the Jewish people is crucial to understanding the Hellenistic apology. It is important to remember that Julian's polemic was not primarily an attack on Jewish cultural and political achievements, but rather more fundamentally a comparison of the God of the Christians with the gods of the Hellenistic world. While their God "bestowed on the Hebrews nothing considerable or of great value," other nations were reaping the benefits given to them by their gods. The achievements of Hellenistic culture argued for the superiority of the pagan gods against the God of the Christians.

To be sure, the emperor was critical of Jewish culture, and for this reason it has been argued that Julian could not have been a friend of the Jews. Whatever positive remarks he might have made about them, it is argued, must be seen in light of their anti-Christian purpose. For example, Julian's overtures toward the Jews in the attempted rebuilding of the Jerusalem temple were based not upon any admiration or sympathy for the Jewish people but out of spite for the Christians. While this observation is correct to a certain extent, it must be remembered that Julian's criticism of the Jews in *Against the Galileans* was every bit as conditioned by his anti-Christian agenda as was his project of rebuilding the temple. In other words, if Julian's pro-Jewish temple project cannot be taken at face value in the context of anti-Christian politics, then neither can his anti-Jewish remarks be interpreted at face value in the parallel context of anti-Christian polemic. Thus his remarks belittling Jewish cultural achievements are to be seen as first and foremost an anti-Christian polemic device; they are not in themselves indicative of a negative attitude toward the Jewish people. A surface reading yields little more than a decontextualized exercise in Roman anti-Judaism.

Julian's comparison of Hellenistic with Jewish achievements is neither primarily anti-Jewish nor merely incidental to his criticism of Christianity. Rather, it constitutes the rhetorical climax of his anti-Christian polemic. The comparison served to form a polemic boundary between Hellenism and what Julian believed was an inferior culture; he accomplished the apology for Hellenism by marginalizing the alternative. Julian was a man steeped in history and in classical literature, proud of Roman might and of Greek culture and desperately afraid for the fate of both. It was the gods who were responsible for the greatness of Hellenistic civilization; it was Christian exclusivism, manifested in the form of a local Palestinian usurper, that was responsible for its decline.

At the same time, we see in Julian's criticism of the "inferior culture" of the Jews and Christians a rhetorical approach based on a strategy of assimilation. He did not universally exclude the Jews, as did Celsus; on the contrary, he welcomed them into the fold of Græco-Roman paganism. To Julian, Judaism represented those aspects of Christianity that could safely be assimilated: confined to a particular people and location, stripped of both universalism and exclusivism, affiliated with an inferior culture, its god reduced to his proper place in the pantheon. In this way Julian could marginalize his opponent, putting Christianity in its rightful place. The season of Celsus' totalizing discourse had ended long ago. Julian's discourse of assimilation, based as it was upon new political realities, was perhaps the most effective anti-Christian rhetorical strategy the times could have offered.

7

Negotiating the Pagan-Christian Divide

This book has been a study of boundaries. Boundaries are what separate "them" from "us" in the discourse of everyday living as well as ritual, of prejudice as well as reason, of rumor as well as intellectual exchange. In the first three centuries of the church, Christian exclusivism was an important element in all of these contexts.

In many ways exclusivism represents the boundary *par excellence*. A dividing line defined largely by negation, Christian exclusivism was easily identifiable in the "pluralistic" religious world of the Mediterranean basin. It took on many forms, the most obvious of which, at least until the end of the second century, was social; theological exclusivism was merely the impetus for its more visible manifestations. The Christians' refusal to participate in civic and domestic cult made them stand out prominently. From the pagan perspective, meetings held in secret, strange rites, and other "boundary markers" simply accentuated the differences. Before Celsus, social exclusivism was the primary pagan objection to Christianity; expressed in terms of accusations of gross immorality, these charges constituted "boundary reinforcements" from the pagan side, propaganda whose purpose was to strengthen the characterization of Christians as radically "other."

Beginning with Celsus, however, theological and philosophical considerations began to assume a more important role. Discussions regarding the reality and providential activity of the gods, the nature of the supreme deity, issues of epistemology, and the relationship of Christianity to Judaism, to name a few, took center stage from the beginning of the third century onward. Together, these and other theoretical concerns formed a conceptual core for the criticisms of all three of our polemicists.

If Christian theology was responsible for creating and maintaining the boundary, the goal of the pagan polemicists was to control its shape, dimensions and strength. In our examination of Celsus, Porphyry and Julian, we detect two major strategies to that end.

The first was to emphasize the differences between Christianity and paganism; such was the approach of Celsus. In the *True Doctrine* we find a totalizing discourse in which no aspect of Christianity was acceptable; Celsus condemned the Christians from every possible perspective. Christianity's social values were incompatible with those of pagan culture; Christian doctrine contradicted Platonic philosophy; Christian origins were objectionable because they were Jewish. Jesus, the apostles, the Bible, Christian preaching and worship all came under Celsus' attack without nuance.

As we examined his arguments against Christianity, particularly those touching on Christian exclusivism, we discovered that although Celsus believed in a kind of "pagan universalism," such a belief unequivocally excluded both Judaism and Christianity. In addition, his consistent association of Christianity with Judaism in a negative manner revealed his desire to marginalize both. The rhetorical boundaries he constructed were firm, leaving as few points of contact as possible between Christianity and the values of mainstream pagan culture. Christians and their doctrines were as distant from the "true doctrine" as Celsus could conceive.

Such a strategy makes sense when we consider the world view of the Græco-Roman intellectual. Christianity represented the perfect rhetorical counterpoint to the values of Roman society. When speaking to an audience that considers itself pious, philosophical and traditional, what better strategy to marginalize your opponents than to characterize them as impious, unphilosophical and innovative? Of course, this strategy did not originate with Celsus. The characterization of Christians as anti-social and impious atheists goes back at least to the early second century and probably before. To take another example, it has been argued[1] that the rhetoric of cannibalism was a historical stereotype, and that the accusation as applied to the Christians had much in common with the alleged cannibalism of a number of disruptive persons and movements throughout the ancient Mediterranean world. This particular accusation, as well as those of ritual infanticide and indiscriminate sex, was an expression of the fear of societal dissolution and cultural collapse. These charges provide examples prior to Celsus of a rhetorical marginalization of Christianity using the stark representation of boundaries.

What Celsus had in common with such earlier accusations was the strategy of representing Christians as completely "other." The fact that he did not employ the charges of cannibalism does not mean that his strategy of marginalization was any different. Instead, he crafted the strategy in other language, primarily that of Platonic philosophical assumptions and standard Græco-Roman piety.

The observation that pagans represented Christianity and their beliefs in complete opposition to pagan values is not a matter of controversy. What is new in our approach is determining the basis and strategy of the rhetoric. Historically, readers of the pagan critics have assumed that they were largely correct, that Christianity was indeed wholly different from the other religions of the Mediterranean. On the other hand, a critical approach to the polemicists leads to a deconstruction of sorts with regard to the literature. By characterizing Christians and their doctrines as "other," pagan critics were not accurately describing the situation; rather, they were attempting to shore up the crumbling walls between Christianity and paganism. What Averil Cameron has observed with regard to Christian writers was just as true for their pagan counterparts.

> Indeed, the prominence of the notion of the *difference* between Christian and pagan expression in the work of the Christian writers themselves is to be read as a rhetorical device and a symptom of adjustment rather than as a description of a real situation.[2]

There was a significant amount of tension between Celsus' strategy of radical exclusion and the reality of Christian social and intellectual integration at the turn of the third century. Thus Celsus' motive was at least as much to create and sustain such difference rhetorically as it was to accentuate actual differences between paganism and Christianity.

We have observed the strategy of creating rhetorical difference, then, as the first approach the pagan critics used to control the boundary between Christianity and paganism. We have also presented it as the dominant approach of Celsus and of the accusations that preceded him in the second century. The second strategy the polemicists used was to identify areas of similarity between Christianity and paganism in order to attack Christian exclusivism. As stated in the first chapter of this book, this later strategy of finding and exploiting points of contact was by no means a concession to Christianity; a rhetoric of exclusion is not the only possible way to marginalize an opponent. Instead of distinctly separating every facet of Christianity from the realm of acceptability, the strategy of assimilation drew boundaries within Christianity itself by noting and accentuating contradictions in Christian belief.

We witnessed this approach in the polemic of both Porphyry and Julian. When the oracles of Apollo and Hecate, according to Porphyry, admitted the soul of Jesus into the company of immortal heroes, it did more than simply change the pagan representation of Jesus from the deceiver and magician of Celsus' polemic to the status of semi-divine being. Porphyry's oracular pronouncements, by characterizing Christ as a pious individual, attempted to create a rhetorical division between Jesus and the Christians who worshiped him. This was not a step toward the approval of Christianity on the part of Porphyry or anyone else. Instead, by shifting the boundary from a location between paganism and Christianity to a location within the Christian belief system, Porphyry continued to deny his opponents any claim to legitimacy. The act of assimilating an element of Christian belief into paganism was an attempt to manage the contours of the pagan-Christian relationship to the disadvantage of the Christians; in this case, to separate Christians from the Christ they worshiped. The same broad strategy holds true for Julian's polemic, particularly his rhetorical assimilation of Judaism within the family of Græco-Roman paganism. Both in his anti-Christian rhetoric and in his policies, his aim was to assimilate his opponents' deity into the pagan universe. By creating a place for the Jewish and Christian God that would be acceptable to pagans, Julian was trying to strike a blow to Christian uniqueness, theological exclusivism, and ultimately Christian political power.

Thus in the polemic of Porphyry and Julian we see a rhetorical—and, in the case of Julian's temple project, political—strategy of assimilation. These later critics marginalized Christianity by incorporating those aspects that would be acceptable to pagan sensibilities and by constructing and identifying contradictions and inconsistencies within Christianity itself. Whether by Porphyry's universalism that would include Christ while excluding the Christians or by Julian's state religion that would ultimately make the Christian God a minor deity in a greater paganism, the rhetorical shift represents a substantive change of strategy from that of Celsus in the attempt to marginalize Christianity.

When and why did this change take place? If it is at all possible to date such a shift, it is evident that it occurred between the writing of Celsus and that of Porphyry, that is, between about 200 and 270 CE. It was during this time that monumental changes took place within both Christianity and paganism. In addition to experiencing dramatic numerical growth, Christianity began, at the turn of the century, appropriating seriously the heritage of Græco-Roman culture. While this appropriation occurred in the area of philosophical theology, it also happened on a popular level as converts to Christianity brought their pagan culture with them into the church. Paganism meanwhile continued its centuries-old process of consolidation and syncretism, a process that would eventually find ways of consciously incorporating elements of Christian thought. The convergence of these factors made possible a degree of rhetorical assimilation that would probably have been unthinkable before the early third century of the Common Era.

The shift from a totalizing discourse to a rhetoric of assimilation is in some ways symptomatic of the similarities between paganism and Christianity, the "common property" held by both sides as discussed in Chapter One. Through the course of this book we have touched on specific examples of these similarities, from Celsus' parallels between Asclepius and Jesus (even in the context of a totalizing discourse) to Porphyry's "Hellenization" of Christ and Julian's "domestication" of the Jewish and Christian God. These examples indicate discrete points of correspondence between pagan and Christian, points that pagan critics used in their attempt to marginalize their opponents.

But the importance of similarity between paganism and Christianity goes beyond the identification of specific examples. The larger issue of similarity lies at the heart of the pagan-Christian conflict and the ultimate inability of pagans to marginalize their opponents successfully. Our present task is to discuss the relationship between the issue of similarity and the strategies of pagan opposition.

One way this relationship can be viewed is by comparing the pagans' anti-Christian polemic and persecution with the pagan treatment of the Jews. Why was it the case that the pagan reaction to Christianity was significantly more violent than the response to Judaism? Although the Jews had many of the same "objectionable" characteristics as the Christians, they were not subjected to the same level of antagonism. For example, the five "objectionable" characteristics of Judaism catalogued in one study[3]—"origins, strangeness, religion and ritual, exclusiveness and proselytizing"—were largely applicable to Christianity as well. This being the case, why did the Christians pose a greater perceived threat to the empire and to society than did the Jews? While a comprehensive answer to this question is not the primary object of this study,[4] some of the suggestions offered here will at least partially explain the more violent attempts to marginalize Christianity as well as the rhetorical strategies involved.

The key to understanding the difference in the pagan reaction to Christianity vis-à-vis Judaism is recognizing the success the pagans generally enjoyed in their efforts to marginalize the Jews to the fringes of Græco-Roman society. If the effective marginalization of a minority group is a necessary step in removing their potential threat to the dominant society, pagans were relatively successful with regard to the Jews. Christianity, on the other hand, was never successfully marginalized, despite attempts on the part of both the pagan critics and the state.

Why did the pagans succeed in marginalizing one group and not the other? In the first place, the Jews represented a distinct ethnic minority within the empire. Whether or not an official "Jewish charter" granting them special status ever actually existed,[5] such ethnic and national identification worked to their advantage since the Romans historically tolerated the religions of the peoples they conquered. Thus Judaism as a religious practice was connected, as far as pagans were concerned, with a specific nationality. And while the status of the Jews as ethnic minority did not prevent their being an object of suspicion and scorn, it did, for the most part, maintain the peace with Rome and prevent large-scale religious persecution.[6]

Christians, on the other hand, could not be marginalized in this manner since they eventually came to represent an ethnic cross-section of the empire. Gentile Christians were not, nationally or ethnically, "other," a fact that made it more difficult to construct a convenient social boundary around them. As a consciously trans-ethnic universalism, Christianity was able to transcend national identity although it lost in the process the protection that such identity afforded the Jews. We see this problem exploited most clearly in Celsus' theology of divine overseers for each nation. Without a national deity, Christians had no god at all, a construct that exposed them to the charge of atheism.

If the first difference between Jews and Christians was the intrinsic difference of ethnicity, the second was an accident of history. There appear to have been significant differences in the intellectual environment of Judaism of the first century CE and that of the fourth century, differences that sharpen the contrast between Judaism and Christianity in terms of pagan efforts to marginalize them. In the first century we witness an active exchange between Judaism and Hellenistic culture and philosophy. Philo of Alexandria was able to flourish in such an environment, creating a fusion of Jewish and Greek thought, and allegorizing the Hebrew Bible to make it acceptable to Hellenistic sensibilities. However, particularly after the revolts of 70 and 135 CE, this interaction was less vigorous. Over the course of the next few centuries, Judaism consolidated its teachings in a less Hellenized manner and was transformed into what would become "normative" Rabbinic Judaism; Philo's project of Hellenization would not be taken up again until the Middle Ages.[7]

Christian intellectuals, on the other hand, aggressively promoted the integration of their theology with Hellenistic culture and learning from the last quarter of the second century onward. Nor was this a phenomenon limited to philosophical circles; the movement included the appropriation of Græco-Roman piety as well. Tertullian's efforts to insulate Christian morality from pagan influence were unsuccessful in the long term; his own conversion to the more ethically rigorous Montanist movement about the beginning of the third century is symptomatic of a larger convergence occurring between Christian and pagan culture. Although the monastic movement would later provide a vehicle for stricter morality and asceticism, it would be primarily an option for the Christian "spiritual elite" and not for the masses. For most Christians, then, the bridge from pagan virtue to Christian morality was neither long nor difficult to cross, while Christian intellectual activity ensured the Christian-ization of Hellenism as well as the Hellenization of Christianity. Thus the cultural boundary between pagans and Christians, relatively firm in the first and second centuries, collapsed over the course of the third.

Therefore Christianity was resistant to marginalization for all the reasons that Judaism was not: Christians were ethnically representative of the population of the empire, while from the late second century onward they successfully assimilated themselves into Græco-Roman culture. These ethnic, behavioral and intellectual characteristics served to minimize, rather than accentuate, the differences between Christianity and the dominant society. The Christians' assimilation of pagan culture made them much more difficult to marginalize than the Jews had ever been.

Thus in many ways it is the difficulty caused by similarity, not by difference, that constitutes one of the keys to understanding the pagan opposition to Christianity. Because of these similarities Christianity could not be marginalized except by force, which was in fact applied with varying intensity and effect until shortly after Constantine began eliminating the distinction between church and empire.

The observation that Christianity's similarities to paganism made the religion more difficult to marginalize suggests that the pagan critics were at least as concerned with the similarities between Christianity and paganism as they were with Christianity as a religion characterized by difference. This is especially the case as the conceptual "bridges" between Christianity and paganism shortened significantly over the course of the third and fourth centuries. The major difference between Celsus and the later critics was the way in which they handled the similarities. The tactic of Celsus was to deny them outright and to exaggerate Christianity as "other"; Porphyry and Julian exploited the similarities in a rhetorical strategy of assimilation. Although differing in approach, both tactics were driven by the need to exercise some measure of control over the public image of Christianity; after all, the wolf in sheep's clothing is much more dangerous than the wolf that looks like a wolf.

By the end of the third century the only remaining boundary of any substance was Christian exclusivism. As a result, this characteristic served as the focus for pagan polemicists in their attempt to push Christianity out of the mainstream into which it had infiltrated; it was Christian exclusivism that, so to speak, made the wolf a wolf. The problem became for the critics: how is it possible to push Christianity out to the margins of Græco-Roman society, isolating it to a point where it will no longer be dangerous? Their answer lay largely in controlling the boundary of Christian exclusivism. Exposing, attacking, and manipulating this boundary became, in the end, their only hope. The pagan polemicists' efforts to control the boundary and the differing strategies they employed to that end has been the subject of this book. Paradoxically, it is the very attempt to manipulate this boundary that reveals many of the points of contact between Christianity and paganism, particularly as the polemic evolved from a totalizing discourse to a strategy of assimilation.

Christianity succeeded in part because it was able to assimilate in many ways to Græco-Roman culture and religion. One of the primary tasks of the critics was to counter this advance by attacking and controlling the boundary of Christian exclusivism. In the end, of course, they were not successful. Why they failed, and why as a result the Roman Empire made the transition from a "pluralistic" paganism to an exclusive universalism, is the logical next question—a question beyond the scope of this book.

Early in this study we remarked that Christianity emerged from Jewish and pagan parents. As a result, the traditional construction of the "boundary" between paganism and Christianity is itself open to question; after all, other traditional designations in the study of Christian antiquity are also coming under increasing scrutiny. These include the bifurcation of "orthodoxy" and "heresy" during the pre-conciliar period,[8] as well as that of "Judaism" and "Christianity" during the first century, particularly before 70 CE.[9] It is possible that the traditional presentation of Christianity as completely different from paganism[10] is simply a residue from the history of Christian scholarship. Historians from Eusebius to the twentieth century have focused on the theme of "conflict," even as this study has. Whether the rise of Christianity has been presented as a contest between the kingdom of God and the power of Satan, a conflict between Christianity and classical culture,[11] or between the church and pagan religion, scholars have traditionally preserved a more or less firm distinction between the opponents. However, this differentiation is becoming increasingly ambiguous.

Even the category of "exclusivism" may not have been the firm and paradigmatic boundary between Christianity and paganism that this book has postulated. After all, a vast number of Christians sacrificed to the gods at the order of Decius, a demonstration of the weakness of the Christian side of the boundary. We have noted

Constantine's own ambiguous relationship to the exclusivist requirements of his new faith, an ambiguity that was at least tacitly accepted
by the church leadership of his time. Christians could be, when
conditions called for it, tolerant of breaches in the barrier.

Nor did such breaches end with Constantine. Paganism continued as a social and intellectual force for at least two more centuries
in the east, while in the west Germanic, Celtic and other paganisms
continued as viable alternatives to Christianity long after the collapse of Roman rule.[12] In such an environment it was sometimes
necessary for Christian evangelists to employ pagan means for Christian ends. Early in the fifth century the Christian Paulinus of Nola
penned the praises of animal sacrifice at the tomb of Saint Felix,
appropriating a traditional pagan rite for the purpose of converting
rural Italians to Christianity.[13] As the demands of conversion less-
ened, so did the strength of Christian exclusivism. Augustine's
rebuke to North African Christians is revealing in this regard: "Let
no man say, 'I go indeed to the idols, I consult possessed ones and
fortune-tellers: yet I abandon not God's Church; I am a Catholic.'"[14]
By the fifth century, at least, the boundary had become permeable
indeed.

Thus if exclusivism formed the boundary *par excellence* between
Christians and pagans, it was nevertheless a boundary that was susceptible to manipulation by Christians and pagans alike for various
ends. The parameters of Christian exclusivism, traditionally assumed to be an immovable barrier, were in fact open to negotiation
from both sides. It is these negotiations that provide some of the
most intriguing information available regarding the world view common to pagans and Christians in late antiquity.

Notes

CHAPTER 1

1. Rodney Stark, *The Rise of Christianity* (Princeton, NJ: Princeton University Press, 1996).
2. Acts 14:16–17.
3. Averil Cameron, *Christianity and the Rhetoric of Empire: The Development of Christian Discourse* (Berkeley: University of California Press, 1991).
4. Theodore S. de Bruyn, "Ambivalence Within a 'Totalizing Discourse': Augustine's Sermons on the Sack of Rome," *Journal of Early Christian Studies* 1/4 (1993): 406.
5. Tertullian *Apology*, trans. Rudolph Arbesmann, Emily Joseph Daly, and Edwin A. Quain, Fathers of the Church, Volume 10 (New York: Fathers of the Church, Inc., 1950) 1.7.
6. Pliny the Younger *Epistles*, 2 volumes, trans. William Melmoth, LCL edition (Cambridge, Mass.: Harvard University Press, 1915, repr. 1940) 10.96.
7. Eusebius *Ecclesiastical History*, trans. Christian Frederick Cruse (New York: T. Mason & G. Lane, 1839; reprint, Grand Rapids: Baker Book House, 1991) 5.1.
8. Pliny the Younger *Epistle* 10.96.
9. Athenagoras *A Plea for the Christians*, trans. B. P. Pratten, ANF collection, Volume 2 (Edinburgh: T&T Clark, 1885; reprint, Grand Rapids: Wm. B. Eerdmans, 1989) 3.
10. Theophilus of Antioch *To Autolycus*, trans. Robert M. Grant (Oxford: Clarendon Press, 1970) 3.4.
11. Galen, Arabic fragment, quoted in Stephen Benko, "Pagan Criticism of Christianity During the First Two Centuries A.D.," *Aufstieg und Niedergang der römischen Welt* (ANRW) II-23.2, ed. H. Temporini and W. Haase (Berlin, 1980), 1099.

CHAPTER 2

1. *Acts of the Scillitan Martyrs*, in H. Musurillo, ed., *The Acts of the Christian Martyrs* (Oxford: Clarendon Press, 1972), 86–89.

2. Tertullian *On the Shows*, trans. S. Thelwall, ANF collection, Volume 3 (Edinburgh: T&T Clark, 1885; reprint, Grand Rapids: Wm. B. Eerdmans, 1989) 24.
3. Harold Remus, "Outside/Inside: Celsus on Jewish and Christian *Nomoi*," in Jacob Neusner et al., eds., *Religion, Literature and Society in Ancient Israel* (Lanham, MD: University Press of America, 1987), 136–7.
4. For an attempt to trace Celsus' arguments through later pagan writers see Georg Loesche, "Haben die späteren Neuplatonischen Polemiker gegen das Christenthum das Werk des Celsus benutzt?" *Zeitschrift für wissenschaftliche Theologie* 27 (1883): 257–302.
5. Origen *contra Celsum*, in *Origen: Contra Celsum*, trans. Henry Chadwick (Cambridge: Cambridge University Press, 1953) preface 4.
6. Ibid. 8.69.
7. Ibid. 8.71.
8. Chadwick, *Origen: Contra Celsum*, xxviii.
9. So argued by J. B. Lightfoot, *The Apostolic Fathers*, part II, volume 1 (New York: Macmillan, 1889-1890, repr. Grand Rapids: Baker Book House, 1981), 530–1, although he advocated a date in the reign of Antoninus Pius (138–161 CE).
10. *contra Celsum* 8.71.
11. Chadwick, *Origen: Contra Celsum*, xxvii.
12. Some of the limitations of *contra Celsum* 8.71 in dating the *True Doctrine* are rightly pointed out by H.-U. Rosenbaum, "Zur Datierung von Celsus' ΑΛΗΘΗΣ ΛΟΓΟΣ," *Vigiliae Christianae* 26 (1972): 102–111.
13. Robert J. Hauck, "Omnes *Contra Celsum?*" *The Second Century* 5/4 (1986): 211–212.
14. The genuineness of this decree is still being debated. Against its authenticity see T. D. Barnes, "Legislation Against the Christians," *Journal of Roman Studies* 58 (1968): 40–41. For arguments in favor, as well as a good summary of the issues surrounding the debate, see W. H. C. Frend, "Open Questions Concerning Christians and the Roman Empire in the Age of the Severi," *Journal of Theological Studies* 25 (1974): 333–351.
15. *contra Celsum* 1.1, 1.3.
16. Ibid. 8.21, 24.

17. Many church historians take Celsus' presentation at face value. See for example W. H. C. Frend, *The Rise of Christianity* (Philadelphia: Fortress Press, 1984), 178; Robert L. Wilken, *The Christians as the Romans Saw Them* (New Haven, CT: Yale University, 1984), 117–125; Henry Chadwick, *The Early Church* (London: Penguin Books, 1967), 54–55, 68.

18. To my knowledge there is no book-length treatment of the subject in English. The best presentations are found in David Rokeah, *Jews, Pagans and Christians in Conflict* (Jerusalem: Magnes Press, 1982) and in his 1968 doctoral dissertation at Hebrew University, titled היהודים בפולמוס הפאגאני-נוצרי מראשיתו ועד לקיסר יוליאנוס (*The Jews in the Pagan-Christian Polemic from its Beginnings to the Emperor Julian*).

19. George Foot Moore's theory that the Jewish figure in the literature was nothing more than "a man of straw" ("Christian Writers on Judaism," *Harvard Theological Review* 14/3 [1921]: 198) has been echoed more recently by Rosemary Radford Ruether, *Faith and Fratricide: The Theological Roots of Anti-Semitism* (Minneapolis: Seabury, 1974), 120.

20. The existence of some kind of dialogue in the pre-Constantinian era is gaining increasing acceptance. Harnack assumed virtually no contact between the church and synagogue by the middle of the second century (*Die Altercatio Simonis Judaei et Theophili christiani, nebst Untersuchungen über die anti-jüdische Polemik in der alten Kirche* [Berlin, 1883]). More recently it has been argued that contact continued at varying levels, and that the continuation of the disputation literature into the Middle Ages is at least as much due to the vitality of Jewish resistance to Christianity as to the need for continuing Christian self-definition; see Marcel Simon, *Verus Israel: A Study in the Relations Between Christians and Jews in the Roman Empire (135–425)*, trans. H. McKeating (Oxford: Oxford University Press, 1986), 138–146, and Amos B. Hulen, "The 'Dialogues with the Jews' as Sources for the Early Jewish Argument Against Christianity," *Journal of Biblical Literature* 51 (1932): 58–70. At the same time it has become clear that the pre-Constantinian dialogues and *adversus Judaeos* literature were written with a pagan audience in the background; see Erwin R. Goodenough, *The Theology of Justin Martyr* (Jena: Verlag Frommannsche Buchhandlung, 1923; reprint, Amsterdam: Philo

Press, 1968); Jon Nilson, "To Whom is Justin's 'Dialogue with Trypho' Addressed?" *Theological Studies* 38/3 (1977): 538–546; and Harold Remus, "Justin Martyr's Argument with Judaism," in Stephen G. Wilson, ed., *Anti-Judaism in Early Christianity*, Volume 2 (Waterloo, Ontario: Wilfrid Laurier University Press, 1986), 59–80.

21. *contra Celsum* 4.23.
22. David Rokeah, "The Jews in the Pagan-Christian Polemic from its Beginnings to the Emperor Julian," *Immanuel* 2 (1973): 62–63.
23. *contra Celsum* 1.2.
24. Ibid. 3.5.
25. Ibid. 1.14.
26. Justin *Dialogue with Trypho*, trans. M. Dods, ANF collection, Vol. 1 (Edinburgh: T&T Clark, 1885; reprint, Grand Rapids, MI: Wm. B. Eerdmans, 1989) 43.
27. *contra Celsum* 1.28–39.
28. Justin *Dialogue with Trypho* 62.
29. Ibid. 83.
30. *contra Celsum* 1.32.
31. Ibid. 1.28–71.
32. Ibid. 2.1–79.
33. Ibid. 1.49.
34. It has been suggested that Celsus wrote the *True Doctrine* as a direct response to Justin's apologetic writings (Carl Andresen, *Logos und Nomos: Die Polemik des Kelsos wider das Christentum* [Berlin: AKG 30, 1955]). Celsus' dependence on Justin is still being disputed; see Gary T. Burke, "Celsus and Justin: Carl Andresen Revisited," *Zeitschrift für die Neutestamentliche Wissenschaft* 76/1–2 (1985): 107–116.

CHAPTER 3

1. Robin Lane Fox, *Pagans and Christians* (New York: Alfred A. Knopf, 1987), 674–681.
2. Walter Scott, introduction to *Hermetica*, Volume 1 (Boulder, CO: Hermes House, 1982; reprint, Boston: Shambhala Publications, 1985), 14.
3. G. W. Bowersock, *Hellenism in Late Antiquity* (Ann Arbor: University of Michigan Press, 1990), 26–27.

4. Ephesians 4:17–20.
5. Justin *First Apology*, trans. Thomas B. Falls (New York: Christian Heritage, Inc., 1948) 7.
6. *contra Celsum* 1.4. The rhetoric of "newness" is curious here. Given the respect for antiquity so prevalent in both pagan and Christian authors, it is somewhat surprising to see Celsus argue that something belonging to Christian teaching is *not* an innovation.
7. Ibid. 3.55.
8. Justin *First Apology* 21.
9. *contra Celsum* 3.22–43.
10. Ibid. 3.26–33.
11. Ibid. 7.51.
12. Ibid. 4.14.
13. For a discussion of the development of Platonist theology see John Peter Kenney, *Mystical Monotheism: A Study in Ancient Platonic Theology* (Hanover, NH: University Press of New England, 1991).
14. *contra Celsum* 5.14.
15. R. T. Wallis, "The Spiritual Importance of Not Knowing," in *Classical Mediterranean Spirituality: Egyptian, Greek, Roman*, ed. A. H. Armstrong (New York: Crossroad Publishing Company, 1986), 460–480.
16. John Whittaker, "Plutarch, Platonism, and Christianity," in *Neoplatonism and Early Christian Thought: Essays in Honour of A. H. Armstrong*, ed. H. J. Blumenthal and R. A. Markus (London: Variorum Publications, 1981), 50.
17. *contra Celsum* 7.36.
18. See the helpful discussion by Robert J. Hauck, "'They Saw What They Said They Saw': Sense Knowledge in Early Christian Polemic," *Harvard Theological Review* 81/3 (1988): 239–249.
19. 1 Corinthians 1:20–21, 25.
20. Plutarch *On the Obsolescence of Oracles*, trans. Frank Cole Babbitt, Plutarch's *Moralia*, Volume 5, LCL edition (Cambridge, Mass.: Harvard University Press, 1957) 416.
21. *contra Celsum* 8.28, 33.
22. Garth Fowden, *Empire to Commonwealth: Consequences of Monotheism in Late Antiquity* (Princeton, NJ: Princeton University Press, 1993), 38–39.

23. *contra Celsum* 7.70.
24. Robert M. Grant, *Gods and the One God* (Philadelphia: Westminster Press, 1986), 54.
25. Lucius Apuleius *The Golden Ass*, trans. J. Arthur Hanson, LCL edition (Cambridge, Mass.: Harvard University Press, 1989) 11.5.
26. P. G. Walsh, "Apuleius and Plutarch," in *Neoplatonism and Early Christian Thought*, 21–23.
27. Numenius of Apamea, quoted by Eusebius *Preparation for the Gospel*, trans. Edwin Hamilton Gifford (Grand Rapids: Baker Book House, 1981) 9.7.
28. *contra Celsum* 1.14, 5.41.
29. Chadwick's conclusion that the "true doctrine" includes Platonic ethics, a belief in eternal bliss, and iconoclasm (*Origen Contra Celsum* xx-xxi) is insufficiently supported. Although Celsus includes these beliefs in his discussion of parallels to Christianity, his intent in this context is to demonstrate the unoriginality of Christianity, not to describe the content of the "true doctrine."
30. *contra Celsum* 5.25.

CHAPTER 4

1. *Augustan History, Severus Alexander* 29.2, trans. David Magie, LCL edition (Cambridge, MA: Harvard University Press, 1921; reprint 1953). Like many other ancient sources, the *Augustan History* is "generally damned and generally used" (J. Bidez, "Literature and Philosophy in the Eastern Half of the Empire," in S. S. Cook, et al., eds., *The Cambridge Ancient History, Volume 12: The Imperial Crisis and Recovery, A.D. 193–324* [Cambridge: Cambridge University Press, 1939; reprint 1961], 598); although the report of the statues in Alexander Severus' chapel is usually treated with great skepticism, there is no adequate reason to dismiss the story out of hand.
2. Zosimus *Historia Nova*, trans. James J. Buchanan and Harold T. Davis (San Antonio, Texas: Trinity University Press, 1967) 1.37.
3. Eusebius *Ecclesiastical History* 6.41.
4. Ibid. 7.11.
5. Ibid. 7.30.
6. Aurelian's action may rightfully be considered a revitalization of an existing cult. The pre-existence of indigenous sun wor-

ship in Rome and the previous attempt by the emperor Elagabalus in 218 to introduce the Syrian solar cult there are discussed in detail by Gaston H. Halsberghe, *The Cult of Sol Invictus* (Leiden: E. J. Brill, 1972). The relevant details are discussed later in this chapter.

7. Franz Cumont, *Oriental Religions in the Roman Empire* (New York: Dover Publications, 1911, repr. 1956), 205.

8. Porphyry *Life of Plotinus,* in Plotinus *The Enneads,* ed. and trans. Stephen MacKenna, 1-20 (London: Faber and Faber Ltd., 1956) 16.

9. Jerome *Commentary in Daniel,* prologue, in *Corpus Christianorum, Series Latina,* Volume 75A, ed. M. Adriaen and F. Glorie (Turnholti: Typographi Brepols Editores Pontificii, 1964). For further discussion see P. M. Casey, "Porphyry and the Origin of the Book of Daniel," *Journal of Theological Studies* 27/1 (1976): 15–33.

10. Preserved by Jerome *Homily on Psalm 81,* in *The Homilies of St. Jerome,* Volume 1, trans. Marie Liguori Ewald (Washington, D.C.: The Catholic University Press, 1966).

11. T. D. Barnes, "Porphyry *Against the Christians:* Date and the Attribution of Fragments," *Journal of Theological Studies* 24 (1973): 424–442.

12. See the defense of the composition date of 270 by Brian Croke, "The Era of Porphyry's Anti-Christian Polemic," *Journal of Religious History* 13/1 (1984): 1–14.

13. Preserved by Eusebius *Ecclesiastical History* 6.19.

14. There is a possible reference to the subject matter of 1 Corinthians 1:18–2:16 in *contra Celsum* 1.9; a portion of Galatians 6:14 appears in *contra Celsum* 5.65; a misquote of 1 Corinthians 3:19 appears in *contra Celsum* 6.12. For a much more generous assessment of Celsus' knowledge of the New Testament see John Patrick, *The Apology of Origen in Reply to Celsus: A Chapter in the History of Apologetics* (Edinburgh: William Blackwood and Sons, 1892), 86–100.

15. Preserved by Augustine *Epistle* 102.2, trans. Wilfrid Parsons (Washington, D.C.: The Catholic University of America Press, 1964).

16. Justin *First Apology* 46.

17. Julius Africanus, for example, claimed in the third century with obvious pride that Moses antedated "Prometheus, Io, Europa,

the Sparti, the abduction of Proserpine, their mysteries, their legislations, the deeds of Dionysus, Perseus, the Argonauts, the Centaurs, the Minotaur, the affairs of Troy, the labours of Hercules, the return of the Heraclidae, the Ionian migration and the Olympiads." Fragment of Julius Africanus *Chronology*, preserved in Georgius Syncellus, trans. unknown, ANF collection, Volume 6 (Edinburgh: T&T Clark, 1885; reprint, Grand Rapids: Wm. B. Eerdmans, 1989), 134.

18. Melito of Sardis, quoted by Eusebius *Ecclesiastical History* 4.26.
19. Eusebius *Proof of the Gospel*, trans. W. J. Farrar (London: S.P.C.K., 1920; reprint, Grand Rapids: Baker Book House, 1981) 3.7.7.
20. Eusebius *Life of Constantine* 2.19, trans. Ernest C. Richardson, NPNF Collection, Second Series, Volume 1, ed. Philip Schaff and Henry Wace (Edinburgh: T&T Clark, 1890; reprint, Grand Rapids: Wm. B. Eerdmans, 1979).
21. Augustine *City of God*, trans. Henry Bettenson (London: Penguin Books, 1984) 10.32.
22. Porphyry *Life of Plotinus* 23.
23. For a detailed treatment of the Platonists of this period see J. M. Dillon, *The Middle Platonists: A Study of Platonism 80 B.C. to A.D. 220* (London: Gerald Duckworth and Company, 1977).
24. John Peter Kenney, "Monotheistic and Polytheistic Elements in Classical Mediterranean Spirituality," in *Classical Mediterranean Spirituality*, 284–285.
25. Kenney, *Mystical Monotheism*, 101–2.
26. Frederick Copleston, *A History of Philosophy*, Volume 1 (Westminster, MD: Newman Press, 1946; reprint, New York: Doubleday, 1985), 470–472.
27. See the discussion in *The Cambridge Ancient History*, 309, as well as Halsberghe, *The Cult of Sol Invictus*, 139.
28. Fowden, *Empire to Commonwealth*, 51.
29. Ibid.
30. Preserved by Augustine *City of God* 19.23.
31. With the exception of the Stoics, who rejected the continued existence of the individual soul after death; see Clifford Herschel Moore, *Ancient Beliefs in the Immortality of the Soul* (New York: Cooper Square Publishers, 1963), 39–42.
32. See Lewis Richard Farnell, *Greek Hero Cults and Ideas of Immortality* (Oxford: Clarendon Press, 1921), 370.

33. Preserved by Augustine *City of God* 19.23.
34. Ibid.
35. Ibid. For further observations on the relationship of Neoplatonic thought to Jewish theology see Gager, "The Dialogue of Paganism with Judaism," 104–109.
36. Preserved by Augustine *City of God* 19.23.

CHAPTER 5

1. There are a number of biographies of the last pagan emperor of Rome. One of the older standards is J. Bidez, *La Vie de l'Empereur Julien* (Paris: Societé d'édition "Les Belles Lettres," 1930, repr. 1965). The two relatively recent "classics" in English are by Robert Browning, *The Emperor Julian* (London: Weidenfeld and Nicolson, 1975) and G. W. Bowersock, *Julian the Apostate* (Cambridge, Mass.: Harvard University Press, 1978). Two more recent biographies have concentrated on the issues of Julian's philosophy and religious beliefs and their influence upon his political actions. Most influential is Polymnia Athanassiadi-Fowden, *Julian and Hellenism: An Intellectual Biography* (Oxford: Clarendon Press, 1981), a thoughtful work that characterizes Julian's religious life and politics as informed by Neoplatonist monotheism. The debate opened by Athanassiadi-Fowden about the emperor's ideology and motivations has been joined by Rowland Smith, *Julian's Gods: Religion and Philosophy in the Thought and Action of Julian the Apostate* (London: Routledge, 1995), who takes the position that Julian was more a traditional polytheist than a Neoplatonic philosopher.
2. Julian *Letter to the Athenians* 2:249. Citations from Julian's works will henceforth be referenced by volume and page number from the Loeb edition of *The Works of the Emperor Julian*, trans. Wilmer Cave Wright (Cambridge, Mass.: Harvard University Press, 1923, reprinted 1961).
3. Whether Julian actively participated in his acclamation has been a matter of debate. The most thorough investigation of the sources is that of Bowersock, *Julian the Apostate*, 46–54, who argues from the various accounts Julian's complicity in the soldiers' action.
4. Julian *Epistle* 8, 3:25.

5. See for example Anthony Meredith, "Porphyry and Julian Against the Christians," ANRW II-23.2, 1147–8; Diana Bowder, *The Age of Constantine and Julian* (New York: Harper & Row Publishers, 1978), 110; Giuseppe Ricciotti, *Julian the Apostate*, trans. M. Joseph Costelloe (Milwaukee: Bruce Publishing Company, 1960), 232.

6. Athanassiadi-Fowden, *Julian and Hellenism*, 161.

7. Historians have traditionally singled out Diocletian as the instigator of the Great Persecution, although Lactantius (the primary source for the persecution) reports that Galerius was the driving force (*On the Deaths of the Persecutors*, trans. Mary Francis McDonald, Fathers of the Church, Volume 54 [Washington, D.C.: Catholic University of America Press, 1965] 9-11). It has been argued against Lactantius that Diocletian was in fact the author of the persecution, and that Lactantius' attribution of the anti-Christian decrees to Galerius was an apologetic convention designed to demonstrate that only "bad emperors" persecuted Christians (P. S. Davies, "The Origin and Purpose of the Persecution of AD 303," *Journal of Theological Studies* 40/1 [1989]: 66–94).

8. There are two accounts of the story. Lactantius' account of the dream in *On the Deaths of the Persecutors* 44 is the earlier and probably more reliable version. Eusebius' more extraordinary account of a vision in the sky with a cross surrounded by the words "By This Conquer" dates from after Constantine's death and is found in the *Life of Constantine* 1.28.

9. The literature on Constantine's conversion and his subsequent Christian beliefs is exceptionally vast. Ever since Jacob Burckhardt characterized Constantine as a political opportunist wholly disinterested in matters of personal religion (*The Age of Constantine the Great*, trans. Moses Hadas [New York: Pantheon Books, 1949]), the debate surrounding the emperor's motives and personal religious beliefs has raged unabated. While Paul Keresztes' *Constantine: A Great Christian Monarch and Apostle* (Amsterdam: J. C. Gieben, 1981) is an extremely traditional view of Constantine's sincerity and Christian piety, most modern scholars have taken various positions in the middle. A. H. M. Jones in *Constantine and the Conversion of Europe* (New York: Macmillan, 1949) retains the theme of political opportunism but

characterizes the emperor's religion as a personal pact with his protector deity. An emperor confused about his religious identity is presented by J. H. W. G. Liebeschuetz in *Continuity and Change in Roman Religion* (Oxford: Clarendon Press, 1979). Other moderating views are presented by Timothy Barnes in *Constantine and Eusebius* (Cambridge, Mass.: Harvard University Press, 1981) and by Michael Grant in *The Emperor Constantine* (London: Weidenfeld & Nicholson, 1993), who argue that Constantine's religious "conversion" was indeed a genuine psychological experience and that his subsequent reign reflected a view of himself as the supreme deity's representative on earth.

10. Especially useful for understanding Constantine's continuity with his predecessors is Liebeschuetz, *Continuity and Change in Roman Religion*.

11. Constantine's father seems to have favored the Sun as the deity of choice on his coinage in the West.

12. Thus Bowder's remark that "For some years Constantine seems to have had no idea that adherence to Christianity automatically excluded any pagan attachment" seems quite incredible (*The Age of Constantine and Julian*, 80).

13. *Latin Panegyric* 12.2, in *XII Panegyrici Latini*, trans. and ed. R. A. B. Mynors (Oxford: Oxford University Press, 1964).

14. For a discussion of the ambiguities in the panegyric of Constantine see H. A. Drake, *In Praise of Constantine: A Historical Study and New Translation of Eusebius' Tricennial Orations* (Berkeley: University of California Press, 1975).

15. For a useful summary of the dedication of the city see Vasiliki Limberis, *Divine Heiress: The Virgin Mary and the Creation of Christian Constantinople* (London: Routledge, 1994), 7–29.

16. In late antiquity, Zosimus *Nova Historia* 2.30; more recently, Timothy Barnes, *Constantine and Eusebius*, 222.

17. The account of the pagan elements in the founding of Constantinople is found in the seventh-century *Chronicon Paschale* by John Malalas, trans. Michael Whitby and Mary Whitby (Liverpool: Liverpool University Press, 1989). Timothy Barnes' dismissal of the *Chronicon's* pagan elements as "later legend" (*Constantine and Eusebius*, 222) is problematic since the *Chronicon* was written in a Christian Byzantine empire in which accounts of Constantine are more likely to have been Christianized, not paganized.

18. Such a false statement makes rhetorical sense if the *Life of Constantine* was written more for the benefit of Constantine's sons than as a historical record, and thus for the purpose of indicating what the ideal Christian monarch *ought* to do—in this case, rid the capital of pagan worship altogether.

19. *Theodosian Code*, ed. Clyde Pharr (Princeton: Princeton University Press, 1952) 9.16.1–2, 16.10.1–2.

20. Eusebius *Life of Constantine* 2.60.

21. Ammianus Marcellinus *Res Gestae*, trans. J. C. Rolfe, LCL edition, 3 volumes (Cambridge, Mass.: Harvard University Press, 1939, repr. 1964) 22.4.3.

22. Ibid. 19.10.4.

23. Libanius *Oration*, trans. A. F. Norman, LCL edition (Cambridge, Mass.: Harvard University Press, 1969) 18.23.

24. The scholarly consensus is that Julian had no desire to make martyrs; the minority view that the emperor leaned more heavily toward outright persecution is expressed by Bowersock, *Julian the Apostate*. For a useful discussion of the issues relevant to whether or not Julian ought to be considered a persecutor see Smith, *Julian's Gods*, 207–218.

25. Julian's religious program was an enigma to an earlier generation of scholars who otherwise considered the emperor a "rationalist" on a crusade against Christian "superstition." Harold Mattingly's evaluation is instructive in this regard: "Julian himself boasted of being a philosopher, but his philosophy was shot through with religious mysticism centered round the worship of the Sun-god. In his attacks on the Christian faith he deals some shrewd blows; but it is not unfair to say that, when he expounds his own mysticism, he is no less exposed to rationalistic attack" (*Christianity in the Roman Empire* [New York: W. W. Norton & Company, 1967], 68). What such an evaluation fails to consider is that sun worship was highly compatible with fourth century Greek philosophy. Julian's "rationalism" is the product of the nineteenth and twentieth, not the fourth, century of the Common Era. Julian was in many ways a man of his times.

26. Tertullian *Prescription Against Heretics*, trans. Peter Holmes, ANF collection, Volume 3 (Edinburgh: T&T Clark, 1885; reprint, Grand Rapids: Wm. B. Eerdmans, 1989) 7.

27. Preserved by Socrates Scholasticus *Ecclesiastical History*, trans.

A. C. Zenos, NPNF collection, Volume 2, Second Series, ed. Philip Schaff and Henry Wace (Edinburgh: T&T Clark, 1890; reprint, Grand Rapids: Wm. B. Eerdmans, 1979) 3.23. Julian conveniently overlooked the fact that philosophers had been allegorizing the Greek myths for centuries.
28. Julian *Against the Galileans* 3:385.
29. Julian *Epistle* 36, 3:117–123.
30. Ammianus *Res Gestae* 22.10.7.
31. Adolf von Harnack, *The Mission and Expansion of Christianity in the First Three Centuries*, trans. James Moffatt, 3 volumes (London: Williams & Norgate, 1908), 1:505.
32. Browning, *The Emperor Julian*, 175.
33. Cochrane, *Christianity and Classical Culture*, 266–7.
34. Wilmer Cave Wright, introduction to *The Works of the Emperor Julian*, 3:314.

CHAPTER 6

1. Michael Adler, "The Emperor Julian and the Jews," *Jewish Quarterly Review* 5 (1893): 615. Although veering too far in the direction of Julian as sympathizer, the article is otherwise an excellent survey of the texts relating to the relationship between Julian and the Jews.
2. Yohanan Lewy, "Julian the Apostate and the Rebuilding of the Temple," in *The Jerusalem Cathedra: Studies in the History, Archaeology, Geography and Ethnography of the Land of Israel*, ed. Lee I. Levine (Jerusalem: Yad Izhak Ben-Zvi Institute, 1983), 70–96.
3. John G. Gager, "The Dialogue of Paganism with Judaism: Bar Cochba to Julian," *Hebrew Union College Annual* 44 (1973): 101.
4. David Rokeah, "The Concept of the 'Election of Israel' in the Pagan-Christian Polemic of the Roman Empire," *Immanuel* 11 (1980): 63.
5. For a summary of early Christian responses to the rebuilding and other aspects of the project see Richard A. Freund, "Which Christians, Pagans and Jews? Varying Responses to Julian's Attempt to Rebuild the Temple in Jerusalem in the Fourth Century CE," *Journal of Religious Studies* 18 (1992): 67–93.
6. Athanassiadi-Fowden, *Julian and Hellenism*, 164.
7. Julian *Against the Galileans* 3:321.

8. Ibid. 3:407.
9. Ibid. 3:375–377.
10. Ibid. 3:329–341.
11. Ibid. 3:331.
12. For a discussion of the implications of this tension in Judaism for the study of Christian origins see Daniel Boyarin, *A Radical Jew: Paul and the Politics of Identity* (Berkeley: University of California Press, 1994), 39–40, 57–85.
13. John Chrysostom *Homily 1 Against the Jews*, trans. Wayne A. Meeks and Robert L. Wilken, in Wayne A. Meeks and Robert L. Wilken, eds., *Jews and Christians in Antioch in the First Four Centuries of the Common Era* (Missoula, Montana: Scholars Press, 1978) 1. See also the discussion by Wolfram Kinzig, "'Non-Separation': Closeness and Co-operation between Jews and Christians in the Fourth Century," *Vigiliae Christianae* 45 (1991): 27–53.
14. Julian *Against the Galileans* 3:341.
15. Julian's use of the term is commonly understood by scholars to indicate the social and geographic obscurity of Christian origins (see for example Ricciotti, *Julian the Apostate*, 231, as well as Bowder, *The Age of Constantine and Julian*, 110). While this may be true, the importance of geographical *limitation* inherent in the term should not be lost. This point is properly understood by Athanassiadi-Fowden, who recognizes that Julian used the term to deny the Christians' claim to universality (*Julian and Hellenism*, 161, note 2).
16. Julian *Against the Galileans* 3:347.
17. Ibid. 3:359.
18. Ibid.
19. Marcel Simon, *Verus Israel*, 112.
20. Eusebius *Proof of the Gospel* 1.5.
21. Julian *Against the Galileans* 3:343–5.
22. Ibid. 3:345.
23. Ibid. 3:375.
24. Ibid.

CHAPTER 7

1. Andrew McGowan, "Eating People: Accusations of Cannibalism Against Christians in the Second Century," *Journal of Early*

Christian Studies 2/3 (1994): 413–442.

2. Averil Cameron, *Christianity and the Rhetoric of Empire*, 7.

3. Jerry L. Daniel, "Anti-Semitism in the Hellenistic-Roman Period," *Journal of Biblical Literature* 98/1 (1979): 47.

4. The comparison of pagan actions against Jews and Christians is addressed from the standpoint of Roman law by Simeon L. Guterman, *Religious Toleration and Persecution in Ancient Rome* (London: Aiglon Press, 1951).

5. See the discussion by Tessa Rajak, "Was There a Roman Charter for the Jews?" *Journal of Religious Studies* 74 (1984): 107–123.

6. That the Romans crushed two major Jewish revolts does not constitute a "persecution" but rather a military action.

7. Robert M. Seltzer, *Jewish People, Jewish Thought: The Jewish People in History* (New York: Macmillan Publishing Company, 1980), 213. The traditional paradigm of Jewish "isolation" has come under scrutiny, however; see the discussion by Ephraim E. Urbach, "Self-Isolation or Self-Affirmation in Judaism in the First Three Centuries: Theory and Practice," in E. P. Sanders, ed., *Jewish and Christian Self-Definition* (Philadelphia: Fortress Press, 1981), 269–298.

8. See especially Walter Bauer, *Orthodoxy and Heresy in Earliest Christianity* (Philadelphia: Fortress Press, 1971).

9. Thus the growing literature on the "separation" of Judaism and Christianity; see for example David Flusser, "The Jewish Christian Schism," *Immanuel* 16 (1983): 32–49; Anthony J. Saldarini, "Jews and Christians in the First Two Centuries: The Changing Paradigm," *Shofar* 10/2 (1992): 16–34; Steven T. Katz, "Issues in the Separation of Judaism and Christianity After 70 C.E.: A Reconsideration," *Journal of Biblical Literature* 103/1 (1984): 43–76.

10. "[M]odern scholarship has too often worked within a set of simple binary oppositions: Christian versus pagan." Cameron, *Christianity and the Rhetoric of Empire*, 21.

11. Or "Christian claims as opposed to Classicism"; Cochrane, *Christianity and Classical Culture*, vi.

12. See Richard Fletcher's excellent treatment of the "boundary problems" involved in "Christianizing" the barbarians in *The Barbarian Conversion from Paganism to Christianity* (New York: Henry Holt and Company, 1997).

13. Dennis Trout, "Christianizing the Nolan Countryside: Animal

Sacrifice at the Tomb of St. Felix," *Journal of Early Christian Studies* 3/3 (1995): 281–298.
14. Augustine *Exposition of Psalm 89*, trans. A. Cleveland Coxe, NPNF Collection, Series 1, Volume 8, ed. Philip Schaff (Edinburgh: T&T Clark, 1888; reprint, Grand Rapids: Wm. B. Eerdmans, 1983) 41.

Select Bibliography

Acts of the Scillitan Martyrs. In *The Acts of the Christian Martyrs,* translated and edited by H. Musurillo, 86–89. Oxford: Clarendon Press, 1972.

Adler, M. A. "The Emperor Julian and the Jews." *Jewish Quarterly Review* 5 (1893): 591–651.

Ammianus Marcellinus. *Res Gestae.* Translated by J. C. Rolfe, 3 vols. Loeb Classical Library. Cambridge, MA: Harvard University Press, 1939; reprint, 1964.

Anastos, Milton V. "Porphyry's Attack on the Bible." In *The Classical Tradition: Literary and Historical Studies in Honor of Harry Caplan,* edited by Luitpold Wallach, 421–450. Ithaca, NY: Cornell University Press, 1966.

Andresen, Carl. *Logos und Nomos: Die Polemik des Kelsos wider das Christentum.* Berlin: AKG 30, 1955.

Apuleius, Lucius. *The Golden Ass.* Translated by J. Arthur Hanson. Loeb Classical Library. Cambridge, Mass.: Harvard University Press, 1989.

Aristides. *Apology.* In *The Ante-Nicene Fathers,* vol. 10, edited by Alexander Roberts and James Donaldson, 263–279. Edinburgh: T&T Clark, 1885; reprint, Grand Rapids: Wm. B. Eerdmans, 1989.

Athanassiadi-Fowden, Polymnia. *Julian and Hellenism: An Intellectual Biography.* Oxford: Clarendon Press, 1981.

Athenagoras. *A Plea for the Christians.* In *The Ante-Nicene Fathers,* vol. 2, edited by Alexander Roberts and James Donaldson, 129–148. Edinburgh: T&T Clark, 1885; reprint, Grand Rapids: Wm. B. Eerdmans, 1989.

Attridge, Harold. "The Philosophical Critique of Religion under the Early Empire." In *Aufstieg und Niedergang der Römischen Welt,* Series 2, edited by H. Temporini and W. Haase, 45–78, vol. 16.1. Berlin: Walter de Gruyter, 1980.

Augustine. *City of God.* Translated by Henry Bettenson. London: Penguin Books, 1984.

———. *Epistles.* Translated by Wilfrid Parsons, S. N. D. de N. Washington: Catholic University of America Press, 1964.

———. *Exposition of Psalm 89.* Translated by A. Cleveland Coxe. In *The Nicene and Post-Nicene Fathers,* Series 1, vol. 8, edited by Philip Schaff, 429–441. Edinburgh: T&T Clark, 1988; reprint, Grand Rapids: Wm. B. Eerdmans, 1983.

Barnes, T. D. "Legislation Against the Christians." *Journal of Roman Studies* 58 (1968): 32–50.

———. "Pre-Decian *Acta Martyrum.*" *Journal of Theological Studies* 19 (1968): 509–531.

———. "Porphyry *Against the Christians:* Date and Attribution of Fragments." *Journal of Theological Studies* 24 (1973): 424–442.

———. *Constantine and Eusebius.* Cambridge, Mass.: Harvard University Press, 1981.

Bauer, Walter. *Orthodoxy and Heresy in Earliest Christianity.* Philadelphia: Fortress Press, 1971.

Beatrice, Pier Franco. "Towards a New Edition of Porphyry's Fragments Against the Christians." In *ΣΟΦΙΗΣ ΜΑΙΗΤΟΡΕΣ: Hommage à Jean Pepin,* edited by Marie-Odile Goulet-Caze, Goulven Madec, Denis O'Brien, 347–355. Paris: Institut d'Etudes Augustiniennes, 1992.

Benko, Stephen. "Pagan Criticsm of Christianity During the First Two Centuries A.D." In *Aufstieg und Niedergang der Römischen Welt,* Series 2, edited by H. Temporini and W. Haase, vol. 23.2, 1055–1118. Berlin: Walter de Gruyter, 1980.

Bidez, J. *La Vie de l'Empereur Julien.* Paris: Societé d'édition "Les Belles Lettres," 1930, reprint 1965.

———. "Literature and Philosophy in the Eastern Half of the Empire." In *The Cambridge Ancient History, Volume XII: The Imperial Crisis and Recovery, A.D. 193–324,* edited by S. S. Cook, 571–650. Cambridge: Cambridge University Press, 1939, reprint 1961.

Blackman, E. C. *Marcion and His Influence.* London: SPCK, 1948.

Bonner, Gerald. "The Extinction of Paganism and the Church Historian." *Journal of Ecclesiastical History* 35/3 (1984): 339–357.

Bowder, Diana. *The Age of Constantine and Julian.* New York: Harper & Row Publishers, 1978.

Bowersock, G. W. *Julian the Apostate.* Cambridge, Mass.: Harvard University Press, 1978.

———. *Hellenism in Late Antiquity.* Ann Arbor: University of Michigan Press, 1990.

Boyarin, Daniel. *A Radical Jew: Paul and the Politics of Identity.* Berkeley: University of California Press, 1994.

Browning, Robert. *The Emperor Julian.* London: Weidenfeld and Nicolson, 1975.

Burckhardt, Jacob. *The Age of Constantine the Great.* Translated by Moses Hadas. New York: Pantheon Books, 1949.

Burke, Gary T. "Celsus and Justin: Carl Andresen Revisited." *Zeitschrift für die Neutestamentliche Wissenschaft* 76/1–2 (1985): 107–116.

———. "Celsus and the Old Testament." *Vetus Testamentum* 36/2 (1986): 241–245.

Cameron, Averil. *Christianity and the Rhetoric of Empire: The Development of Christian Discourse.* Berkeley: University of California Press, 1991.

Cary, M. and H. H. Scullard. *A History of the Roman Empire Down to the Reign of Constantine*, 3rd edition. New York: St. Martin's Press, 1975, reprint 1984.

Casey, P. M. "Porphyry and the Origin of the Book of Daniel." *Journal of Theological Studies* 27/1 (1976): 15–33.

Chadwick, Henry. "Origen, Celsus, and the Resurrection of the Body." *Harvard Theological Review* 41/2 (1948): 83–102.

———. *Origen: Contra Celsum*. Cambridge: Cambridge University Press, 1953.

———. *The Early Church*. London: Penguin Books, 1967.

Claudius Mamertinus. *Latin Panegyric*. Translated by Marna M. Morgan. In *The Emperor Julian: Panegyric and Polemic*, 2nd. ed., edited by Samuel N. C. Lieu, 13–38. Liverpool: Liverpool University Press, 1989.

Clement of Alexandria. *The Stromata*. In *The Ante-Nicene Fathers*, vol. 2, edited by Alexander Roberts and James Donaldson, 299–567. Edinburgh: T&T Clark, 1885; reprint, Grand Rapids: Wm. B. Eerdmans, 1989.

Cochrane, Charles Norris. *Christianity and Classical Culture: A Study of Thought and Action from Augustus to Augustine*. New York: Oxford University Press, 1957.

Cook, S. S. et al., ed. *The Cambridge Ancient History, Volume XII: The Imperial Crisis and Recovery, A.D. 193–324*. Cambridge: Cambridge University Press, 1939; reprint 1961.

Copleston, Frederick. *A History of Philosophy*, vol. 1. Westminster, MD: Newman Press, 1946; reprint, New York: Doubleday, 1985.

Croke, Brian. "The Era of Porphyry's Anti-Christian Polemic." *Journal of Religious History* 13/1 (1984): 1–14.

Cumont, Franz. *Oriental Religions in the Roman Empire*. New York: Dover Publications, 1911; reprint 1956.

Cyril of Alexandria. *Contra Iulianum*. In *Patrologia Græca Cursus Completus*, ed. J. P. Migne, 505–1064, vol. 76. Paris: Vivès, 1863.

Daniel, Jerry L. "Anti-Semitism in the Hellenistic-Roman Period." *Journal of Biblical Literature* 98/1 (1979): 45–65.

Davies, P. S. "The Origin and Purpose of the Persecution of AD 303." *Journal of Theological Studies* 40/1 (1989): 66–94.

de Bruyn, Theodore S. "Ambivalence Within a 'Totalizing Discourse': Augustine's Sermons on the Sack of Rome." *Journal of Early Christian Studies* 1/4 (1993): 405–421.

de Ste. Croix, G. E. M. "Why Were the Early Christians Persecuted?" *Past and Present* 26 (1963): 6–38.

———. "Why Were the Early Christians Persecuted? — A Rejoinder." *Past and Present* 27 (1964): 28–33.

Dieu, P. Léon. "La Persécution au IIᵉ Siècle: Une Loi Fantôme." *Revue D'Histoire Ecclesiastique* 38 (1942): 5–19.

Dillon, J. M. *The Middle Platonists: A Study of Platonism 80 B.C. to A.D. 220.* London: Gerald Duckworth and Company, 1977.

―――. "Plutarch and Second Century Platonism." In *Classical Mediterranean Spirituality: Egyptian, Greek, Roman,* edited by A. H. Armstrong, 214–229. New York: Crossroad Publishing Company, 1986.

―――. "Porphyry's Doctrine of the One." In *ΣΟΦΙΗΣ ΜΑΙΗΤΟΡΕΣ: Hommage à Jean Pepin,* edited by Marie-Odile Goulet-Caze, Goulven Madec, and Denis O'Brien, 356–366. Paris: Institut d'Etudes Augustiniennes, 1992.

Dorrie, Heinrich. *Die platonische Theologie des Kelsos in ihrer Auseinandersetzung mit der christlichen Theologie.* Göttingen: Vandehoeck & Ruprecht, 1967.

Drake, H. A. *In Praise of Constantine: A Historical Study and New Translation of Eusebius' Tricennial Orations.* Berkeley: University of California Press, 1975.

Ephrem Syrus. *Hymns Against Julian.* Translated by Judith M. Lieu. In *The Emperor Julian: Panegyric and Polemic,* 2nd ed., edited by Samuel N. C. Lieu, 105–128. Liverpool: Liverpool University Press, 1989.

Eusebius. *The Book of Martyrs.* In Eusebius, *Ecclesiastical History.* Translated by Christian Frederick Cruse, 349–378. New York: T. Mason & G. Lane, 1839; reprint, Grand Rapids: Baker Book House, 1991.

―――. *Ecclesiastical History.* Translated by Christian Frederick Cruse. New York: T. Mason & G. Lane, 1839; reprint, Grand Rapids: Baker Book House, 1991.

―――. *Life of Constantine.* Translated by Ernest C. Richardson. In *The Nicene and Post-Nicene Fathers,* vol. 1, Second Series, edited by Philip Schaff and Henry Wace, 481–559. Edinburgh: T&T Clark, 1890; reprint, Grand Rapids: Wm. B. Eerdmans, 1979.

―――. *Preparation for the Gospel.* Translated by Edwin Hamilton Gifford. Grand Rapids: Baker Book House, 1981.

―――. *The Proof of the Gospel.* Translated by W. J. Ferrar. London: S.P.C.K., 1920; reprint, Grand Rapids: Baker Book House, 1981.

Farnell, Lewis Richard. *Greek Hero Cults and Ideas of Immortality.* Oxford: Clarendon Press, 1921.

Ferguson, John. *The Religions of the Roman Empire.* Ithaca, NY: Cornell University Press, 1970.

Flusser, David. "The Jewish Christian Schism." *Immanuel* 16 (1983): 32–49.

Fowden, Garth. *Empire to Commonwealth: Consequences of Monotheism in Late Antiquity.* Princeton, NJ: Princeton University Press, 1993.

Fox, Robin Lane. *Pagans and Christians.* New York: Alfred A. Knopf, 1987.

Frend, W. H. C. "Open Questions Concerning Christians and the Roman Empire in the Age of the Severi." *Journal of Theological Studies* 25 (1974): 333–351.

———. *The Rise of Christianity*. Philadelphia: Fortress Press, 1984.

———. *The Archaeology of Early Christianity: A History*. Minneapolis: Fortress Press, 1996.

Freund, Richard A. "Which Christians, Pagans and Jews? Varying Responses to Julian's Attempt to Rebuild the Temple in Jerusalem in the Fourth Century CE." *Journal of Religious Studies* 18 (1992): 67–93.

Gager, John G. "The Dialogue of Paganism with Judaism: Bar Cochba to Julian." *Hebrew Union College Annual* 44 (1973): 89–118.

Gamble, H. Y. "Euhemerism and Christology in Origen: *Contra Celsum* III 22–43." *Vigiliae Christianae* 33/1 (1979): 12–29.

Gilliard, Frank D. "Notes on the Coinage of Julian the Apostate." *Journal of Roman Studies* 54 (1964): 135–141.

Goodenough, Erwin R. *The Theology of Justin Martyr*. Jena: Verlag Frommannsche Buchhandlung, 1923; reprint, Amsterdam: Philo Press, 1968.

Goulet-Caze, Marie-Odile, Goulven Madec, and Denis O'Brien, eds. ΣΟΦΙΗΣ ΜΑΙΗΤΟΡΕΣ: *Hommage à Jean Pepin*. Paris: Institut d'Etudes Augustiniennes, 1992.

Grant, Michael. *The Emperor Constantine*. London: Weidenfeld & Nicholson, 1993.

Grant, Robert M. *Gods and the One God*. Philadelphia: Westminster Press, 1986.

———. *Greek Apologists of the Second Century*. Philadelphia: Westminster Press, 1988.

Guterman, Simeon L. *Religious Toleration and Persecution in Ancient Rome*. London: Aiglon Press, 1951.

Halsberghe, Gaston H. *The Cult of Sol Invictus*. Leiden: E. J. Brill, 1972.

Harnack, Adolf von. *Die Altercatio Simonis Judaei et Theophili christiani, nebst Untersuchungen über die anti-jüdische Polemik in der alten Kirche*. Leipzig: J. C. Hinrichs, 1883.

———. *The Mission and Expansion of Christianity in the First Three Centuries*, 3 vols. Translated by James Moffatt. London: Williams & Norgate, 1908.

———. "Porphyrius, 'Gegen die Christen,' 15 Bücher: Zeugnisse, Fragmente und Referate." *Abhandlungen der königlich preussischen Akademie der Wissenschaften*, philosophisch-historische Klasse 1916, nr. 1:1–115.

———. *Marcion: Das Evangelium von fremden Gott*. Darmstadt: Wissenschaftliche Buchgesellschaft, 1960.

Hauck, Robert J. "Omnes Contra Celsum?" *The Second Century* 5/4 (1986): 211–225.

———. "'They Saw What They Said They Saw': Sense Knowledge in Early Christian Polemic." *Harvard Theological Review* 81/3 (1988): 239–249.

Herford, R. Travers. *Christianity in Talmud and Midrash*. London: Williams and Norgate, 1903.

Herodotus. *History.* Translated by A. D. Godley. Loeb Classical Library. Cambridge, Mass.: Harvard University Press, 1981–82.

Hoffmann, R. Joseph. *On the True Doctrine: A Discourse Against the Christians.* New York: Oxford University Press, 1987.

———. *Porphyry's "Against the Christians": The Literary Remains.* Amherst: Prometheus Books, 1994.

Hulen, Amos B. "The 'Dialogues with the Jews' as Sources for the Early Jewish Argument Against Christianity." *Journal of Biblical Literature* 51 (1932): 58–70.

Jerome. *Against the Pelagians.* Translated by John N. Hritzu. In *Saint Jerome, Dogmatic and Polemical Works.* The Fathers of the Church, vol. 53, edited by L. Schopp, 223–378. Washington: Catholic University of America Press, 1965.

———. *Commentariorum in Danielem. Corpus Christianorum, Series Latina,* vol. 75a, edited by M. Adriaen and F. Glorie. Turnholti: Typographi Brepols Editores Pontificii, 1964.

———. *Commentariorum in Matheum. Corpus Christianorum, Series Latina,* vol. 77, ed. D. Hurst and M. Adriaen. Turnholti: Typographi Brepols Editores Pontificii, 1969.

———. *Homily on Psalm 81.* In *The Homilies of St. Jerome,* vol. 1. Translated by Marie Liguori Ewald, 102–110. Washington, D.C.: Catholic University of America Press, 1966.

John Chrysostom. "Homily on Saint Babylas, Against Julian and the Pagans." Translated by Marna M. Morgan. In *The Emperor Julian: Panegyric and Polemic,* 2nd ed., edited by Samuel N. C. Lieu, 59–79. Liverpool: Liverpool University Press, 1989.

———. *Homily 1 Against the Jews.* Translated by Wayne A. Meeks and Robert L. Wilken. In *Jews and Christians in Antioch in the First Four Centuries of the Common Era,* edited by Wayne A. Meeks and Robert L. Wilken, 85–104. Missoula, MO: Scholars Press, 1978.

John Malalas. *Chronicon Paschale.* Translated by Michael Whitby and Mary Whitby. Liverpool: Liverpool University Press, 1989.

Jones, A. H. M. *Constantine and the Conversion of Europe.* New York: Macmillan, 1949.

Julian. *Epistle 8.* In *The Works of the Emperor Julian,* translated by Wilmer Cave Wright, vol. 2, 21–27. Loeb Classical Library. Cambridge, Mass.: Harvard University Press, 1923; reprint 1961.

———. *Epistle 36.* In *The Works of the Emperor Julian,* translated by Wilmer Cave Wright, vol. 3, 117–123. Loeb Classical Library. Cambridge, MA: Harvard University Press, 1923; reprint 1961.

———. *Epistle 51.* In *The Works of the Emperor Julian,* translated by Wilmer Cave Wright, vol. 2, 177–181. Loeb Classical Library. Cambridge, MA: Harvard University Press, 1923; reprint 1961.

————. *The Works of the Emperor Julian*, 3 vols. Translated by Wilmer Cave Wright. Loeb Classical Library. Cambridge, MA: Harvard University Press, 1923; reprint 1961.

Julius Africanus. *Chronology*. Preserved in Georgius Syncellus, *Chronology*. In *The Ante-Nicene Fathers*, vol. 6, edited by Alexander Roberts and James Donaldson, 130–138. Edinburgh: T&T Clark, 1885; reprint, Grand Rapids: Wm. B. Eerdmans, 1989.

Justin Martyr. *Dialogue with Trypho*. Translated by M. Dods. In *The Ante-Nicene Fathers*, vol. 1, edited by Alexander Roberts and James Donaldson, 194–270. Edinburgh: T&T Clark, 1885; reprint, Grand Rapids, MI: Wm. B. Eerdmans, 1989.

————. *First Apology*. Translated by Thomas B. Falls. New York: Christian Heritage, Inc., 1948.

————. *Second Apology*. Translated by M. Dods. In *The Ante-Nicene Fathers*, vol. 1, edited by Alexander Roberts and James Donaldson, 188–193. Edinburgh: T&T Clark, 1885; reprint, Grand Rapids, MI: Wm. B. Eerdmans, 1989.

Katz, Steven T. "Issues in the Separation of Judaism and Christianity After 70 C.E.: A Reconsideration." *Journal of Biblical Literature* 103/1 (1984): 43–76.

Keim, Theodor. *Celsus' Wahres Wort*. Zürich, 1873.

Kenney, John Peter. "Monotheistic and Polytheistic Elements in Classical Mediterranean Spirituality." In *Classical Mediterranean Spirituality: Egyptian, Greek, Roman*, edited by A. H. Armstrong, 269–292. New York, NY: Crossroad Publishing Company, 1986.

————. *Mystical Monotheism: A Study in Ancient Platonic Theology*. Hanover, NH: University Press of New England, 1991.

Keresztes, Paul. *Constantine, A Great Christian Monarch and Apostle*. Amsterdam: J. C. Gieben, 1981.

King, C. W. *Julian the Emperor*. London: George Bell and Sons, 1888.

Kinzig, Wolfram. "'Non-Separation': Closeness and Co-operation between Jews and Christians in the Fourth Century." *Vigiliae Christianae* 45 (1991): 27–53.

Lactantius. *Divine Institutes*. In *The Ante-Nicene Fathers*, vol. 7, edited by Alexander Roberts and James Donaldson, 3–223. Edinburgh: T&T Clark, 1885; reprint, Grand Rapids: Wm. B. Eerdmans, 1989.

————. *On the Deaths of the Persecutors*. Translated by William Fletcher. In *The Ante-Nicene Fathers*, vol. 7, edited by Alexander Roberts and James Donaldson, 301–322. Edinburgh: T&T Clark, 1885; reprint, Grand Rapids, MI: Wm. B. Eerdmans, 1989.

La Piana, George. "Foreign Groups in Rome During the First Centuries of the Empire." *Harvard Theological Review* 20/4 (1927): 183–403.

Lewy, Yohanan. "Julian the Apostate and the Rebuilding of the Temple." In *The Jerusalem Cathedra: Studies in the History, Archaeology, Geography and Ethnography of the Land of Israel*, vol. 3, edited by Lee I. Levine, 70–96. Jerusalem: Yad Izhak Ben-Zvi Institute, 1983.

Libanius. *Selected Works*. Translated by A. F. Norman, 3 vols. Loeb Classical Library. Cambridge, MA: Harvard University Press, 1969.

Liebeschuetz, J. H. W. G. *Continuity and Change in Roman Religion*. Oxford: Clarendon Press, 1979.

Lieu, Samuel N. C., ed. *The Emperor Julian: Panegyric and Polemic*, 2nd ed. Liverpool: Liverpool University Press, 1989.

Lightfoot, J. B. *The Apostolic Fathers*, part II, vol. 1. New York: Macmillan, 1889–1890; reprint, Grand Rapids: Baker Book House, 1981.

Limberis, Vasiliki. *Divine Heiress: The Virgin Mary and the Creation of Christian Constantinople*. London: Routledge, 1994.

Livy. *From the Foundation of the City*. Translated by B. O. Foster et al. Loeb Classical Library. Cambridge, Mass.: Harvard University Press, 1952–1959.

Loesche, Georg. "Haben die späteren Neuplatonischen Polemiker gegen das Christenthum das Werk des Celsus benutzt?" *Zeitschrift für wissenschaftliche Theologie* 27 (1883): 257–302.

MacMullen, Ramsay. *Paganism in the Roman Empire*. New Haven, CT: Yale University Press, 1981.

———. *Christianizing the Roman Empire, A.D. 100–400*. New Haven, CT: Yale University Press, 1984.

———. *Christianity and Paganism in the Fourth to Eighth Centuries*. New Haven, CT: Yale University Press, 1997.

Marcus Aurelius. *Meditations*. Translated by George Long. Danbury, CT: Grolier Enterprises, 1907; reprint, 1980.

Martyrdom of Polycarp. In *The Ante-Nicene Fathers*, vol. 1, edited by Alexander Roberts and James Donaldson, 39–44. Edinburgh: T&T Clark, 1885; reprint, Grand Rapids: Wm. B. Eerdmans, 1989.

Mattingly, Harold. *Christianity in the Roman Empire*. New York: W. W. Norton & Company, 1967.

McCartney, Dan G. "Literal and Allegorical Interpretation in Origen's *Contra Celsum*." *Westminster Theological Journal* 48 (1986): 281–301.

McGowan, Andrew. "Eating People: Accusations of Cannibalism Against Christians in the Second Century." *Journal of Early Christian Studies* 2/3 (1994): 413–442.

Meredith, Anthony. "Porphyry and Julian Against the Christians." *Aufstieg und Niedergang der Römischen Welt*, Series 2, edited by H. Temporini and W. Haase, 1119–1149, vol. 23.2. Berlin: Walter de Gruyter, 1980.

Migne, J. P., ed. *Patrologia Graeca, Cursus Completus*. 161 volumes. Paris: Vivès, 1857–1866.

Minucius Felix. *Octavius*. In *The Ante-Nicene Fathers*, vol. 4, edited by Alexander Roberts and James Donaldson, 173–198. Edinburgh: T&T Clark, 1885; reprint, Grand Rapids: Wm B. Eerdmans, 1989.

Momigliano, A. D. *The Conflict Between Paganism and Christianity in the Fourth Century*. Oxford: Oxford University Press, 1963.

Moore, Clifford Herschel. *Ancient Beliefs in the Immortality of the Soul*. New York, NY: Cooper Square Publishers, 1963.

Moore, George Foot. "Christian Writers on Judaism." *Harvard Theological Review* 14/3 (1921): 197–254.

Nazianzen, Gregory. "Two Invectives Against Julian the Emperor." Translated and edited by C. W. King. In *Julian the Emperor*, edited by C. W. King, 1–121. London: George Bell and Sons, 1888.

Neumann, Karl Johannes. *Kaiser Julians Bücher gegen die Christen*. Leipzig: B. G. Teubner, 1880.

Nilson, Jon. "To Whom is Justin's 'Dialogue with Trypho' Addressed?" *Theological Studies* 38/3 (1977): 538–546.

Origen. *Contra Celsum*. Translated by Henry Chadwick. Cambridge: Cambridge University Press, 1953.

Osborn, Eric Francis. *Justin Martyr*. Tübingen: J. C. B. Mohr, 1973.

Patrick, John. *The Apology of Origen in Reply to Celsus: A Chapter in the History of Apologetics*. Edinburgh: William Blackwood and Sons, 1892.

Pharr, Clyde, ed. *The Theodosian Code*. Princeton, NJ: Princeton University Press, 1952.

Pistorius, Philippus Villiers. *Plotinus and Neoplatonism: An Introductory Study*. Cambridge: Bowes & Bowes, 1952.

Plato. *Apology*. In *Plato*, vol. 1. Translated by Harold North Fowler. Loeb Classical Library. London: Heinemann; New York: Putnam's Sons, 1924.

———. *Epistles*. In *Plato*, vol. 7. Translated by Harold North Fowler. Loeb Classical Library. London: Heinemann; New York: Putnam's Sons, 1930.

Pliny the Younger. *Epistles*, 2 vols. Loeb Classical Library. Translated by William Melmoth. Cambridge, Mass.: Harvard University Press, 1915; reprint 1940.

Plutarch. *On the Obsolescence of Oracles*. Translated by Frank Cole Babbitt. In Plutarch, *Moralia*, vol. 5, 350–501. Loeb Classical Library. Cambridge, Mass.: Harvard University Press, 1957.

Porphyry. *Life of Plotinus*. In Plotinus, *The Enneads*, edited and translated by Stephen MacKenna, 1–20. London: Faber and Faber Ltd., 1956.

Quasten, Johannes. *Patrology*, 4 vols. Utrecht: Spectrum, 1950; reprint, Westminster, MD: Christian Classics, 1992.

Rajak, Tessa. "Was There a Roman Charter for the Jews?" *Journal of Religious Studies* 74 (1984): 107–123.

Reid, J. K. S. *Christian Apologetics*. London: Hodder and Stoughton, 1969.

Remus, Harold. "Justin Martyr's Argument with Judaism." In *Anti-Judaism in Early Christianity*, vol. 2, edited by Stephen G. Wilson, 59–80. Waterloo, Ontario: Wilfrid Laurier University Press, 1986.

———. "Outside/Inside: Celsus on Jewish and Christian *Nomoi*." In *Religion, Literature, and Society in Ancient Israel, Formative Christianity and Judaism*, vol. 2, edited by Jacob Neusner et al., 133–150. Lanham, MD: University Press of America, 1987.

Ricciotti, Giuseppe. *Julian the Apostate*. Translated by M. Joseph Costelloe. Milwaukee, WI: Bruce Publishing Company, 1960.

Roberts, Alexander and James Donaldson, ed. *The Ante-Nicene Fathers*, 10 vols. Edinburgh: T&T Clark, 1885; reprint, Grand Rapids: Wm B. Eerdmans, 1989.

Rokeah, David. היהודים בפולמוס הפאגאני־נוצרי־נוצרי מראשיתו ועד לקיסר יוליאנוס (*The Jews in Pagan-Christian Polemic from Its Beginnings to the Emperor Julian*). Ph.D. dissertation, Hebrew University, 1968.

———. "The Jews in the Pagan-Christian Polemic from Its Beginnings to the Emperor Julian." *Immanuel* 2 (1973): 61–67.

———. "The Concept of the 'Election of Israel' in the Pagan-Christian Polemic of the Roman Empire." *Immanuel* 11 (1980): 56–63.

———. *Jews, Pagans and Christians in Conflict*. Jerusalem: Magnes Press, 1982.

Rosenbaum, H.-U. "Zur Datierung von Celsus' ΑΛΗΘΗΣ ΛΟΓΟΣ." *Vigiliae Christianae* 26 (1972): 102–111.

Ruether, Rosemary Radford. *Faith and Fratricide: The Theological Roots of Anti-Semitism*. Minneapolis, MN: Seabury, 1974.

Saldarini, Anthony J. "Jews and Christians in the First Two Centuries: The Changing Paradigm." *Shofar* 10/2 (1992): 16–34.

Schaff, Philip, ed. *The Nicene and Post-Nicene Fathers*, Series 1, 14 vols. Edinburgh: T&T Clark, 1888; reprint, Grand Rapids: Wm. B. Eerdmans, 1983.

Schaff, Philip and Henry Wace, eds. *The Nicene and Post-Nicene Fathers*, Series 2, 14 vols. Edinburgh: T&T Clark, 1890; reprint, Grand Rapids: Wm. B. Eerdmans, 1979.

Schoedel, William R. "Christian 'Atheism' and the Peace of the Roman Empire." *Church History* 42/3 (1973): 309–319.

Schwartz, Jacques. "Du Testament de Lévi au Discours Véritable de Celse." *Revue d'Histoire et de Philosophie Religieuses* 40/2 (1960): 126–145.

Scott, Walter, ed. and trans. *Hermetica*, vol. 1. Boulder, CO: Hermes House, 1982; reprinted Boston, Mass.: Shambhala Publications, 1985.

The Scriptores Historiae Augustae. Translated by David Magie. Loeb Classical Library. Cambridge, Mass.: Harvard University Press, 1921; reprint 1953.

Sherwin-White, A. N. "The Early Persecutions and Roman Law Again." *Journal of Theological Studies* 3 (1952): 199–213.

―――. "Why Were the Early Christians Persecuted? — An Amendment." *Past and Present* 27 (1964): 23–27.

―――. *The Letters of Pliny: A Historical and Social Commentary.* Oxford: Clarendon Press, 1966.

Simon, Marcel. *Verus Israel: A Study in the Relations Between Christians and Jews in the Roman Empire (135–425).* Translated by H. McKeating. Oxford: Oxford University Press, 1986.

Smith, Rowland. *Julian's Gods: Religion and Philosophy in the Thought and Action of Julian the Apostate.* London: Routledge, 1995.

Socrates Scholasticus. *Ecclesiastical History.* Translated by A. C. Zenos. In *The Nicene and Post-Nicene Fathers,* Second Series, vol. 2, edited by Philip Schaff and Henry Wace, 1–178. Edinburgh: T&T Clark, 1890; reprint, Grand Rapids: Wm. B. Eerdmans, 1979.

Sordi, Marta. *The Christians and the Roman Empire.* Translated by Annabel Bedini. Norman, OK: University of Oklahoma Press, 1986.

Sozomen. *Ecclesiastical History.* Translated by Chester D. Hartranft. In *The Nicene and Post-Nicene Fathers,* Second Series, vol. 2, edited by Philip Schaff and Henry Wace, 239–427. Edinburgh: T&T Clark, 1890; reprint, Grand Rapids: Wm. B. Eerdmans, 1979.

Stötzel, Arnold. "Warum Christus so spät erschein—die apologetische Argumentation des frühen Christentums." *Zeitschrift für Kirchengeschichte* 92/2–3 (1981): 147–160.

Tacitus. *Annals.* Translated by John Jackson. Loeb Classical Library. Cambridge, Mass.: Harvard University Press, 1931; reprint 1962.

Tertullian. *Ad Nationes.* Translated by Peter Holmes. In *The Ante-Nicene Fathers,* vol. 3, edited by Alexander Roberts and James Donaldson, 109–147. Edinburgh: T&T Clark, 1885; reprint, Grand Rapids: Wm. B. Eerdmans, 1989.

―――. *Apology.* Translated by Rudolph Arbesmann, Emily Joseph Daly, and Edwin A. Quain. Fathers of the Church, vol. 10. New York: Fathers of the Church, Inc., 1950.

―――. *On the Shows.* Translated by S. Thelwall. In *The Ante-Nicene Fathers,* vol. 3, edited by Alexander Roberts and James Donaldson, 79–91. Edinburgh: T&T Clark, 1885; reprint, Grand Rapids: Wm. B. Eerdmans, 1989.

―――. *Prescription Against Heretics.* Translated by Peter Holmes. In *The Ante-Nicene Fathers,* vol. 3, edited by Alexander Roberts and James Donaldson, 243–267. Edinburgh: T&T Clark, 1885; reprint, Grand Rapids: Wm. B. Eerdmans, 1989.

Theophilus. *To Autolycus.* Translated by Robert M. Grant. Oxford: Clarendon Press, 1970.

Against the Christians

Urbach, Ephraim E. "Self-Isolation or Self-Affirmation in Judaism in the First Three Centuries: Theory and Practice." In *Jewish and Christian Self-Definition*, edited by E. P. Sanders, 269–298. Philadelphia, PA: Fortress Press, 1981.

Vogt, J. *Kaiser Julian und das Judentum*. Leipzig: J. C. Heinrichs, 1939.

Wallis, R. T. "The Spiritual Importance of Not Knowing." In *Classical Mediterranean Spirituality: Egyptian, Greek, Roman*, vol. 15, edited by A. H. Armstrong, 460–480. New York: Crossroad Publishing Company, 1986.

Walsh, Joseph J. "On Christian Atheism." *Vigiliae Christianae* 45 (1991): 255–277.

Walsh, P. G. "Apuleius and Plutarch." In *Neoplatonism and Early Christian Thought: Essays in Honour of A. H. Armstrong*, edited by H. J. Blumenthal and R. A. Markus, 20–63. London: Variorum Publications, 1981.

Watson, Gerard. "Celsus and the Philosophical Opposition to Christianity." *Irish Theological Quarterly* 58/3 (1992): 165–179.

Whittaker, John. "Plutarch, Platonism, and Christianity." In *Neo-platonism and Early Christian Thought: Essays in Honour of A. H. Armstrong*, ed. H. J. Blumenthal and R. A. Markus, 50–63. London: Variorum Publications, 1981.

Wilken, Robert L. *The Christians as the Romans Saw Them*. New Haven, CT: Yale University, 1984.

Wolff, G. *Porphyrii de philosophia ex oraculis haurienda*. Berlin: AKG, 1856.

Workman, Herbert B. *Persecution in the Early Church*. Publisher unknown, 1906; reprint, Oxford: Oxford University Press, 1980.

Wright, Wilmer Cave. "Introduction to *Against the Galileans*." In *The Works of the Emperor Julian*, vol. 3, translated by Wilmer Cave Wright, 313–317. Loeb Classical Library. Cambridge, Mass.: Harvard University Press, 1923; reprint 1961.

XII Panegyrici Latini. Translated and edited by R. A. B. Mynors. Oxford: Oxford University Press, 1964.

Zosimus. *Historia Nova*. Translated by James J. Buchanan and Harold T. Davis. San Antonio, Texas: Trinity University Press, 1967.

Index

Abraham, 65

Adam, 75

Aemilianus, 66

Against the Christians. See Porphyry, *Against the Christians*

Against the Galileans. See Julian, *Against the Galileans*

Alexander the Great, 126

Alexander Severus, 65, 71

Alexandria, 19, 23, 63–66, 100

allegory, 101, 115

Ammianus, 102

anthropomorphism, 101, 114, 117

Antioch, 67, 92, 110

Antiochus Epiphanes, 69

antiquity, as cultural value, 7, 74–75, 108, 110, 123

Antonine dynasty, 18

Apollo, 39, 87, 99, 132

apologetic, 4, 14, 17, 22–23, 75–77, 115; and Christian morality, 42–43; and pagan gods, 5, 44–46, 49; and similarity to paganism, 3, 44–46

apostasy, 111; from Judaism, 59, 108, 111, 122; from paganism, 59, 108, 111

Apuleius, 56–57, 83

Asclepius, 6, 44–46, 49, 60, 83, 125, 133

assimilation, rhetoric of. *See* rhetorical strategy

Athanassiadi-Fowden, Polymnia, 93

atheism, atheists, 5, 13–14, 130, 135

Athenagoras, 14

Athens, 27, 65, 85, 101

Augustan History, 65, 87

Augustine, 74, 77–78, 88, 138

Augustus (Caesar), 76, 89, 97

Augustus (imperial office), 92, 94–96

Aurelian, 67-68, 82–83, 89, 94, 100

Balkans, 95

barbarians, 34, 53, 65, 111

Basil, 101

Bible. *See* scriptures

Bithynia, 9

Bosporus, 96

boundaries, rhetorical, 2–4, 48, 50, 60–61, 90, 107, 127, 129–132

Britain, 94

Byzantium, 97

cannibalism, 12–14, 17, 22, 43, 60, 63–64, 130

Caesar (imperial office), 13, 92, 94–95

Caesarea (Cappadocia), 99

Cameron, Averil, 7, 131

Caracalla, 83

Carpus, 12

Carthage, 17, 23, 65

Celsus, 1, 17–64, 65–66, 72, 86, 93–94, 106–107, 109–110, 131–133; and the Bible, 74; date of his work, 20–24, 135; as an informed critic, 20, 22, 32, 62; interpretation of polemic, 2, 62; use of Judaism, 31–40, 44, 115;

rhetorical strategy, 41, 48, 62–64; social criticism, 24–31; as source of later arguments, 70–71; universalism of, 59–61, 63

Cenchreae, 56

Chadwick, Henry, 21

Christ. *See* Jesus

Christianity: conversion to, 23, 63, 67; and philosophy, 1, 3, 6–7, 48–49, 63, 101, 116–117, 133; recent appearance of, 73–77, 89, 107, 123–125; relationship to Judaism, 1, 7–9, 15, 30–32, 75, 111, 115–119, 129–130, 133–136; relationship to paganism, 1–8, 27, 30, 41–50, 60, 88–89, 96–103, 130–139; and Roman Empire, 7, 29–30, 63–67, 75–77, 89, 95; and society, 18–19, 24–25, 28–30, 59–61, 63–67, 71, 96–99, 129; success of, 1, 100, 137

Chrysopolis, 96

Church of the Holy Sepulchre, 122

Clement of Alexandria, 19, 23, 47, 59, 61, 101

coinage, 97, 103

Commodus, 17, 21

Constans, 99

Constantine, 16, 61, 76–77, 83, 91, 94–100, 103, 136, 138

Constantine II, 99

Constantinople, 92, 97–98

Constantius Chlorus, 94

Constantius II, 91–92, 96, 99

contra Celsum. See Origen, and *contra Celsum*

conversion, 23, 28, 59, 63–65, 88, 91, 115, 133

creation, 37, 112–115

Cumont, Franz, 68

Cyprian, 65

Cyril of Alexandria, 92

Dacia, 67

daemons, 5, 26, 54–56

Daniel, book of, 69

Danube, 29

Decius, 29, 63–67, 86, 88–89, 137

Delphi, 39, 84

Dialogue with Trypho, 32, 36–38

difference, rhetoric of. *See* rhetorical strategy, of difference

Diocletian, 94–95

Dionysius, 66

Dionysus, 45

disciples of Jesus, 52, 69–70, 72–73

Discussion Between Jason and Papiscus, 37

divinity: of emperors, 84; of Jesus, 44–46, 132; of people, 84–85

Domitian, 9, 11

Dura Europos, 71

Egypt, Egyptians, 35–36, 41, 44, 56–58, 66–67, 111, 125

Elagabalus, 82

Emesa, 64, 82

epistemology, 48, 51–53, 129

eschatology, 42, 72

Eusebius, 12, 47, 76, 83, 97–98, 123, 137

exclusivism, 31, 97, 113; ambiguity as a boundary, 137–138; defined, 6; pagan objection to, 6–7, 41–42, 45–46, 66, 73–77, 83, 88, 117, 124, 129–132; political, 77; of prophecy, 38; social, 7, 24–30, 35, 71, 89, 129; theologi-

cal, 25, 129, 132
Felix, Saint, 138
Fronto, Cornelius, 12–14
Gaius Caesar, 74
Galen, 14
Galerius, 94–95
Gaul, 67, 92; persecution in, 12–13,
 17, 21–22, 28–29, 61
Germans, 29, 118
Gnostics, Gnosticism, 9, 69
gods, 10, 38, 41, 43, 44–46, 85–86,
 126; images of, 10, 42, 97; as
 national overseers, 58–59, 107,
 115–118, 123, 135; and nature, 5,
 55–56; origin of, 113–114; as
 preservers of peace, 10; and
 public events, 18, 24–26, 28, 54,
 58; as subordinate to God, 26–
 27, 56–59; worship of, 10, 13,
 26, 54–56, 59, 66, 81, 92
Goths, 63, 67
Great Persecution, 70, 95
Harnack, Adolf von, 69, 104
Hebrew Bible, 30, 35–37, 39, 71–72,
 108
Hecate, 84–85, 132
Helios, 100, 125
Hellenism, 1, 5–7, 48, 107, 111, 113–
 115, 120, 135; Christian
 appropriation of, 15–16, 93,
 101–102
Hellenistic apology, 93–94, 103, 111,
 115, 125–127
Heracles, 45
Hermes, 83
heroes, 84
hetaeria, 25
Hezekiah, 37

Hippocrates, 126
Hymn to King Helios, 100
Hymn to the Mother of the Gods, 100
immorality: as accusation against
 Christians, 12–15, 17, 20, 22, 60,
 63–64, 102, 129–131; as accusation against pagans, 42–44
impassibility, 25–26
imperial cult, 82
incarnation, 48–50, 68, 117
incest, 12, 17
informants, 10–11, 15
insanity, 85–86
Isis, 56–58, 75, 83
Jerusalem, 8, 31, 65, 101, 121–122,
 126
Jesus, 65, 67, 75–76, 97, 117, 123–124;
 Christian worship of, 4, 6, 45,
 85, 88, 112, 132; comparison
 with gods, 3, 38, 44–46, 49, 60,
 133; crucifixion, 44, 68, 73;
 ethics of, 42–44; as founder of
 Christianity, 15; immortalized
 by pagan oracle, 72–73, 83–88,
 123, 132; as magician and
 sorcerer, 34–35, 83–84, 87, 132;
 resurrection of, 6, 45, 68, 73, 84
"Jewish charter," 134
Jewish Law, 31–32, 75, 110–111, 116
Jewish scriptures. *See* Hebrew Bible
Johannine literature, 52
John Chrysostom, 116
Jovian, 92
Judaism: in anti-Christian polemic,
 30–40, 58, 71–72, 107–123;
 arguments against Christianity,
 36–40; conversion to, 23; as
 ethnic minority, 134–136;

relationship to Christianity (*see* Christianity, relationship to Judaism)

Julia Domna, 64

Julia Mamaea, 65

Julian, 2–4, 20, 30, 48, 60, 91–127, 129, 132; *Against the Galileans,* 92–94, 103–105, 113, 119–120; against Christian teachers, 91, 102–103; comparison with Celsus and Porphyry, 8, 31, 92–94, 103–105, 107–108, 111, 123, 125, 132–133; and Hellenism, 93–94, 103, 114–115, 125–127; interpretation of, 103–105, 109–110, 115; and the Jews, 33–34, 107–115, 121–122, 125–127; life of, 91–92; and "pagan church," 100–101; rhetorical strategy, 105, 107, 115; temple project, 109–110, 121–122, 126, 132

Julius Africanus, 145 n. 17

Jupiter, 44, 81, 83, 86

Justin Martyr, 3, 26, 44–46, 75, 84, 107, 124; and Christian morality, 43; and Jewish-Christian dialogue, 32, 36–38; and Platonism, 47, 89, 101, 116

Lactantius, 148 nn. 7, 8

Laodicea, 12

Licinius, 95–96

Life of Constantine, 76

Lyons, 12, 14, 21–22

Madaura, 12

magic: disciples and, 69–70; Jesus and, 84, 87; pagan, 98

manumission, 96

Marcion, Marcionite movement, 9, 31, 59, 116, 118

Marcus Aurelius, 12, 17, 21, 29, 65, 76; and Christian apologetic, 17; mention of Christians, 17

marginalization, 4, 8, 35, 53, 59–60, 94, 120, 127, 130–136

Martyrdom of Perpetua and Felicitas, 22

Maxentius, 94–97

Maximian, 94–95

Maximin Daia, 94

Maximinus, 95

Melito of Sardis, 76

Mercury, 44, 83

Mesopotamia, 92

Middle Platonism, 79

Milvian Bridge, battle of, 95

miracles, 6

Mithraism, 75

monotheism, 111; Christian, 4–5, 26, 30, 54, 59; pagan, 4, 55–59

Montanism, 9, 18–19, 135

Moses, 34–35, 39, 75, 111, 114, 117–119

mythology, 113–115; Christian, 46; pagan, 6, 38, 42–46, 54

Neoplatonism, 47, 51, 63–64, 68, 79–81, 91, 100, 109

Neptune, 83

Nero, 9–10, 29

New Testament, 31, 69–73, 119

Numenius, 57–58

Old Testament. *See* Hebrew Bible

On the Return of the Soul, 78

oracle, 70, 72, 80, 84–85, 87–88, 132

Origen, 18–19, 26, 60, 63–65, 71, 76; and Christian philosophy, 50, 89, 101; and *contra Celsum,* 19–

21, 23, 27, 30, 35–39, 45, 60, 63, 108

Orpheus, 65

overseers. *See* gods, as national overseers

Palestine, 124

Pantera, 37, 39

Papylus, 12

Paris, 92

Paul, apostle, 31, 52–53, 69, 72, 75, 117, 119

Paul of Samosata, 67

Paulinus of Nola, 138

Pergamum, 12

persecution, 3, 9, 11, 17–19, 20–22, 59, 64, 96, 100, 133–134; imperial, 63, 65–66, 70, 95; popular, 10–15, 22, 28–29, 100

Perseus, 44

Persia, Persians, 65, 92, 110

Philip the Arab, 65

Philo, 135

philosophy, 71, 114; Christian appropriation of, 1, 6–7, 15–16, 19, 40, 47–49, 59, 61, 63, 89, 101, 116–117, 133; pagan use against Christians, 24, 47–54, 72–73, 124; and universalism, 78–82

Philosophy from Oracles, 70, 79, 87

Plato, 3, 40, 43, 47–48, 51–52, 55, 57, 61, 78–79, 89, 113–114

Pliny the Younger, 9–12, 25

Plotinus, 51, 63, 79–80, 91

Plutarch, 57, 83

political theology, 76

Polycarp, 12–15

polytheism, 3–5, 54–59, 81, 114

pontifex maximus, 97

Porphyry, 2–3, 20, 30, 60, 63–90, 91–92, 103–104, 107–108, 132–133; *Against the Christians*, 68–72, 82, 93, 104; comparison to Celsus, 68–73, 81–83, 86–87, 89; criticism of Jesus, 87; on the book of Daniel, 69; on immortality of Jesus, 72–73, 83–88, 123, 132; and Judaism, 71–72; use of philosophy, 72–73; rhetorical strategy, 72; universalism of, 77–82

Poseidon, 83

Proof of the Gospel, 76

propaganda, 12, 14, 17, 28–30

prophecy, 38–39, 41, 121

proselytizing, 24, 27, 43–44, 134

providence, 5

rebellion, as characteristic of Christians, 27

resurrection: of the dead, 42, 50–51, 54, 70, 72; of Jesus, 6, 45–46, 68, 84

revelation, 46–47

Rhea, 97

rhetorical strategy, 24, 109; of assimilation, 3, 89–90, 94, 103, 107, 115, 121–123, 127, 131–133, 136–137; changes in, 2–3, 7–9, 31, 34, 64, 87, 89, 132–133, 137; of difference, 2–3, 30, 39–40, 59–61, 130–131

Rome, 9, 65–68, 74, 82, 95

sacrifice, 10, 13, 15, 25, 64–66, 92, 95, 98–99, 108, 110–111, 121–122, 137–138

Sagaris, 12

Sapor I, 65

Saturninus, Vigellius, 17
Scilli, 12, 17, 21, 29
scriptures, 19–20, 69–70, 85, 95, 101–
    102, 108, 113–114, 117, 119, 130
Scythians, 42, 58
Septimius Severus, 18, 22–23, 64
Severan dynasty, 18, 59, 64, 83, 87,
    89
Severus (4th-century Caesar), 94–95
Smyrna, 12–14
sociology, and success of Christian-
    ity, 1
Socrates (Greek philosopher), 27, 43
Socrates (church historian), 69
Sol Invictus, 68, 82–83, 89, 97, 100
Solomon, 126
soothsaying, 98
Sophocles, 85
Stark, Rodney, 1
syncretism, 68, 74, 82–83, 89, 97, 133
Syria, 67, 74, 82, 92
Tacitus, 9
Talmud, 37
Tatian, 3
temple: Jewish, 109–111, 121–122,
    126, 132; pagan, 98–100, 112
Tertullian, 40, 61, 101; apologetic, 3,

9, 22–24; and Christian
    morality, 18–19, 28, 135
tetrarchy, 94–96
Theodosius I, 96
Theophilus, 14
"third race," Christians as, 1
Timaeus, 52, 112–114
Torah. *See* Jewish Law
totalizing discourse, 7–8, 14, 30, 40,
    46, 60, 86, 89, 127, 130–131, 133,
    137
Tower of Babel, 118, 121
Trajan, 10–11, 13, 15, 25
Tricennial Oration, 97
Tyche, 97
universalism: Christian, 31, 74, 89,
    116–120, 121, 124, 134; Jewish,
    31, 116, 124, 127; pagan, 56–59,
    61, 73, 75–83, 89–90, 130, 132
Valerian, 66–67
Vienne, 12, 21–22
virgin birth, 36–38
Zen, 58
Zenobia, 67
Zeus, 58, 81, 83, 99, 125
Zoroaster, 69
Zosimus, 65

Patristic Studies

This is a series of monographs designed to provide access to research at the cutting-edge of current Patristic Studies. Particular attention will be given to the development of Christian theology during the first five centuries of the Church and to the different types of Biblical interpretation which the Fathers used. Each study will engage with modern discussion of the theme being treated, but will also break new ground in original textual research. In exceptional cases, a volume may consist of the critical edition of a text, with notes and references, as well as translation. Revised doctoral dissertations may also be published, though the main focus of the series will be on more mature research and reflection. Each volume will be about 250–300 pages (100,000–120,000 words) long, with a full bibliography and index.

Inquiries and manuscripts should be directed to:

Peter Lang Publishing
Acquisitions Department
516 N. Charles Street, 2nd Floor
Baltimore, MD 21201

To order other books in this series, please contact our Customer Service Department at:

(800) 770-LANG (within the U.S.)
(212) 647-7706 (outside the U.S.)
(212) 647-7707 FAX

or browse online by series at:

www.peterlang.com